Dhows

Dhows
David Howarth

Photographs by Robin Constable

Quartet Books
London . Melbourne . New York

First published
by Quartet Books Limited 1977
A member of the Namara Group
27 Goodge Street, London WIP IFD

ISBN 0 7043 2148 3

Design by Mike Jarvis / Jim Wire

Printed in Great Britain by
Gavin Martin Limited, Wallington, Surrey

Contents

Fisherman: lateen sails come in all sizes

Dugouts have been imported from India since Sumerian times

Palm frond boat

Introduction

In 1976, I went to call on a very distinguished Arab in Bahrain in the Arabian Gulf, and said I believed he knew Naim Attallah. 'Naim?' he said. 'Oh yes, he was in here the other day – as usual, with three hundred new ideas in the first two minutes.'

I had met Naim Attallah for the first time in London a few weeks before, and had the same experience: he fired off a salvo of new ideas. This book was one of them. He is a publisher, among many other things, and he asked me to go to Arabia and write about dhows, the ancient sailing ships of Arabian seas. It took me about another two minutes to say I would.

Like many other people, I find pleasure in wooden ships and boats, their history and the art and craft of designing, building and sailing them. Dhows are particularly fascinating. Among them are the biggest wooden ships that are still being built, and the oldest kinds of seagoing ships that are still in use. They work on trade routes that have existed for 4500 years. They were doing it, much the same as they are now, at the time of Trafalgar, at the time of the Spanish Armada, at the time of the Norman Conquest – even at the time of Christ, and possibly at the time of Noah's Ark.

I had been in Arabia before, and noticed then that different kinds of dhows have a very surprising resemblance to the ships of different eras long ago in northern European history. Some are like early medieval relics, and none are more modern in design than the 17th century. To a student of ships, it was like discovering a lost world where dinosaurs and pterodactyls were still alive and well. It was not a new discovery: I learned that other people had noticed it too. But in reading and writing since then about the history of ships, I had often wanted a chance to have another look at dhows, and see how they fitted into the history of the sea and how they came to be built the way they are, unique in the modern world.

There was a good reason for making a record now, in text and pictures, of these archaic ships: their aeon of existence may be nearly ended. In the modern Arab world they seem pathetically out of date. There are still some places in Arabia, desert creeks and fishing villages, where dhows do not look out of place; but in others, the little mud-walled towns that have suddenly sprouted into concrete cities, it is very strange to see such ancient ships across the street from the new hotels and international banks and office blocks. They are still being built exactly the same as they have been for centuries past – except that they all have engines now; but it is a question how much longer they can find an economic trade to keep them going. If they fail, they will disappear very suddenly.

So we set off to see them. There is nothing adventurous now in Arabian travel: remembering what it used to be like, it seems absurdly easy, and Naim's arrangements made it luxurious. But it is also absurdly expensive. To keep the cost of producing this book within any reasonable limits, we chose sample places for our photographic tour, and most of the pictures, as things turned out, were taken in the Arabian Gulf and on the coast of Oman. But by hunting around, we found almost all the kinds of dhows that exist, and I hope I have done justice to the other centres of dhow traffic, which extend all round the coast of Arabia from Kuwait to Suez.

It was an enjoyable journey. I had not been there since 1961, when I was writing the biography of ibn Saud, the founder of the modern Kingdom of Saudi Arabia. At that time it seemed the ancient values of the desert Arabs, their dignity, asceticism and probity, were being drowned and lost in the flood of oil money. Indeed, the old King had died distressed by that belief. Certainly those values have evolved, but now it seems they have survived and even been enhanced and spread by wealth. Prosperity, after a bad start, has filtered down through Arab society, even to those who used to be desperately poor, and has overflowed to the immigrants from Pakistan and India who far outnumber the native Arabs in some of the oil states. So now the most humble people, more prosperous than they ever dreamed of being, are cheerful, sure of themselves, apparently free of envy, and outstandingly friendly and courteous to strangers. Heaven knows what will happen to their new-built cities in the end; but at present it is a pleasure to meet such optimism and ebullience. Everyone was kind to us – everyone from the high officials of governments to the sailors on dhows and the workers in boatyards, and the people we casually met on the way – like the men who appeared from nowhere in the heat of an afternoon and set to work with enormous enthusiasm and dug our car out of the sand where we had stuck it, and then disappeared again almost before we could thank them.

I hope some of them will see this product of our journey, and accept our thanks now for the generous welcome they gave us.

Acknowledgements

The pictures on pages 51 and 54 are by Jo White; they are drawn in oil pastel on an oil monotype base.
The author and publishers also thank the Governments of the United Arab Emirates and Bahrain; H. E. Tariq Almoayyed; Zaki Nusseibeh; Khalifah Shaheen; the many captains of dhows and master builders in boatyards who gave their patient help; Mr Patrick Board of Intercontinental Hotels; Angela Johnstone for help with the line drawings; Major John Stewart Smith for the photograph on page 111; the National Maritime Museum, Greenwich; and Messrs Allen and Unwin for permission to reproduce the drawing on page 24.

History and before

One has to begin by admitting that dhow is a bogus word. Any European sailor knows what it means and can picture a dhow in his mind's eye – a brown teak hull, a poop deck, a long raking stem and a lateen rig, sailing on the coasts of Arabia and the Indian Ocean. The spelling of dhow, the initial dh, makes it look like a transcription of an Arabic word. But it is not. No Arab sailor thinks of his ship as a dhow: it is a baggala, a boom, a sambuk, a shu'ai – he has a dozen different words for different kinds of dhows. The origin of the word is mysterious. There are claims that it is Swahili, or an Indian corruption of the name of a Chinese ship, or a derivative of a word *tava* which is used in a 15th-century Russian manuscript to describe a ship of something like this kind. To me, the dh suggests it is one of the many 'native' words the British adopted during their rule of India, perhaps from a misunderstanding of a local dialect. The Oxford Dictionary of Etymology traces it back no farther than the 19th century, and no English–Arabic dictionary I have seen includes it at all. But I have used it as the title of this book because there is no better word that means quite the same thing.

Some kinds of dhows are built and used all down the west coast of India, and down the east coast of Africa as far as Mozambique. But in this book we are concerned with the dhows of Arabia itself, because that is where they began and where they still have the centre of their existence – the Red Sea, the Arabian Gulf and the coast of Muscat.

This part of the world was the scene of very early civilizations: the Red Sea leads up to Egypt, and the Gulf leads up to Babylonia and Sumeria. It is also a place where human change, after those civilizations vanished, was exceptionally slow, until the discoveries of oil transformed it. Twenty-five years ago, people were living in its deserts exactly as they lived in early Biblical times, and a few of them are still doing so now. And not only its deserts: at sea also, in those thousands of years, life went on the same.

On the journey we made in 1976 to take the photographs for this book, we came upon a sight which seemed to me to epitomize that strange stagnation. We were driving up the coast of the Gulf of Oman in the south-east corner of Arabia. This is a place that few European explorers had seen a generation ago: but we were on one of the first-class roads that the riches of oil have built, and only a short morning's drive from the international airport of Dubai. I had read of a very primitive kind of boat that was said to exist on that shore, and we had been poking about in fishing villages hoping to find one. Suddenly, when we did not expect it, there it was: a huge empty sandy beach, the barren mountains of Oman behind, and in the middle, miles from anywhere, a little boat made entirely of the fronds of date-palms.

This is the most ancient of boats. The Egyptians made the same kind of thing from reeds and the marsh Arabs of Mesopotamia do it still; but there are no reeds in southern Arabia, only palms. The shell of the boat was palm fronds, sewn with palm fibres on to sticks that acted as frames. The deck was the same, and it had deck beams – but they were laid on top of the decking, not under it, to hold the decking down rather than hold it up, and they were sewn right through the bottom of the boat. The whole of the inside, under the deck, was carefully packed with the husks that are left on the trunk of a date-palm when the dead fronds are cut off. It was not built like most boats to keep the water out, but merely to be as buoyant as possible with the water inside it.

It was a prehistoric relic which made the whole scene look like a diorama in a museum. But it was new. There was nobody in sight, but somebody had paddled it ashore there from the open ocean and hauled it up on the sand, spread out his fishing nets to dry, and stored in the boat some useful flotsam he had found on the beach, including lumps of expanded polystyrene. It could have been built just the same, without any tools, in any era of human evolution; but the fronds and bindings were fresh, and I judged it was built last winter.

That little boat could not be called a dhow, but it illustrated the changelessness of seafaring in Arabia; and there is one kind of dhow which also appears to be prehistoric. This is the boom – which incidentally is the largest of dhows that are still being built. Just as the palm-frond boat is the oldest, most primitive thing made to carry a man on the water, so the boom is the primeval essence of a cargo-carrying ship. All the other big dhows evolved from it when Arabs first saw European ships, but that evolution happened a mere three or four hundred years ago. The boom is a far more ancient creation. Its design goes back at least eight hundred years and, I suspect, for thousands of years before that.

•

I shall describe the different kinds of dhows in a later chapter: here I shall only mention the ultimate simplicity of the boom. It can be quite a big ship, up to 200 feet in length – bigger than a Nelsonian frigate and not far short of an 80-gun ship of the line. It is built like all dhows entirely of Indian teak, and like all primitive ships it is double-ended. The keel is one straight log, the stem is another and the sternpost is a third. The stem and sternpost have such a rake that the keel is only about half the length of the ship. A boom has one deck, set very low in the ship so that half the cargo is carried on top of it, and there is a short poop deck above it in the stern. The only conspicuous decoration is a very large extension of the stemhead. A boom looks like the kind of ship small children draw – the kind one can make by folding a sheet of paper. It has the cumbrous air of a mythical sea-monster.

There is a reason for building a ship this way. Arab shipwrights to this day seem reluctant to make a keel from two logs joined in the middle. I may be wrong to generalize, and one cannot very often see the keel of a big dhow; but I have never seen one that is not in one piece. Nowadays, they could easily make a strong enough joint if they wanted to, but through most of their history they had no iron to make reliable bolts to hold it together. So their keels, I think, have always been the longest single logs they can find; and a boom is simply the largest ship one can build with logs of a limited length.

These ships are built in the Arabian Gulf but not in the Red Sea, and they trade from there down the coasts of Africa and India. It is the trade from the Gulf to India that can be traced to the very beginning of recorded history.

The Sumerians had an elaborate civilization in Mesopotamia at the head of the Gulf 2500 years before Christ, and they were prolific writers. Enormous numbers of their clay tablets have been discovered and deciphered. In the legends they wrote down, a place called Dilmun is prominent. It was the place they believed their ancestors came from, their Garden of Eden, a land of immortality; their story of man's fall is similar to the Biblical story and was written before the book of Genesis. Dilmun was also the home of their Noah, the survivor of their story of the flood. In short, it was already recognized, four and a half millennia ago, as an even more ancient land.

But it was not only a legendary place. Other tablets are business contracts and even letters, addressed to the merchants of Dilmun. Some of them complain, in a homely manner, of shoddy goods and exorbitant prices. Dilmun ships are often recorded in Babylon and Ur, where they loaded cargoes of woollen goods and returned with copper, gold, ivory, rare woods and precious stones. Dilmun is described as an island three days' sail down the gulf from the Mesopotamian cities; and from archaeological evidence in recent years, it has been identified with certainty as the island of Bahrain – which still is one of the centres of dhow traffic and still is conspicuous in the Gulf as a green and fertile place with natural springs.

So the ships came from Bahrain; but their cargoes could not have been local products. They could only have come from India, Africa or the southern coast of Arabia, perhaps from all three, and even the shortest of voyages to fetch them was over a thousand miles.

The three-cornered trade between Sumeria and India, with Bahraini merchants as providers of the shipping, is confirmed by the seals that merchants used to stamp the tablets that recorded their transactions. Sumerian seals were cylindrical: the merchants rolled them on the clay. In the civilization that existed then in the valley of the Indus, the seals were always rectangular. But in excavations at both ends of the trade route, in Sumeria and India, 1600 miles apart, a few round seals were found in recent years. These remained enigmatic until great numbers of them, and a sealmaker's workshop, were unearthed in Bahrain. They were the seals of Dilmun.

This is not the place for archaeological details, but digging in Bahrain has also shown that it survived the rise and fall of empires and remained a prosperous place, under different dynasties of rulers, through almost all the centuries since Sumeria. It was remote, it was a fertile island, and it had something special to offer, a skill in merchant seamanship; it also had riches of its own, even from the time of Sumerian legend, in pearl fisheries, and now it has riches in oil. So it has remained a favoured place, making its recurrent mark in history, for a longer continuous period than anywhere else in the world.

But Bahrain, of course, was never the only Arab port engaged in the eastern trade, and the route through the Gulf was not a monopoly. The Red Sea route was always a competitor, and sometimes dominated the trade.

●

When one comes to think of it, Red Sea is a curious name. No sea is red. To the Romans and Greeks, the whole of the Indian Ocean, including the Gulf, was known as the Red Sea, the Erythraean Sea; and in the origin of the name, the history of Bahrain intrudes again. According to Persian legend, the sea took its name from a ruler named Erythras who lived on its shore. This legend may coincide with an archaeological theory that a mysterious tribe called the Red Men – or the Men of Erythras – migrated from the Biblical land of Elam, which was in Persia, across the Gulf to Bahrain, and settled there and spread right round the coasts of Arabia. Thus it was not the sea itself that was red, but the people who lived on its shore and sailed their ships on it; and in the Red Men we may have the origin not only of the name, but also of the nautical skill of the coastal Arabs.

From this same centre at the head of the Gulf – either Bahrain itself or somewhere very near it – the same remarkable seafaring skill and tradition spread northwards too. The Phoenicians migrated from there to the Mediterranean coast around Tyre and Sidon, and became for many centuries the most successful seamen in the Mediterranean: the race that first sailed out through the Straits of Gibraltar to the Atlantic and carried their seagoing trade as far as the south-west of England.

When King Solomon sent his ships to seek the same exotic cargoes the Sumerians bought, he used the Red Sea route and the ships were built in the Gulf of Akaba. But the seamen who sailed them were Phoenicians, lent to him by King Hiram of Tyre. Other monarchs from the north who wished to send fleets to the southward also called in the Phoenicians. Sennacherib the Assyrian emperor did it in the 7th century B.C., bringing Phoenician sailors and shipwrights, and probably their timber too, overland to Nineveh. Alexander did the same, and transported the ships themselves in sections from the Mediterranean coast to the river Euphrates.

But none of these Mediterranean seamen penetrated beyond the mouths of the Red Sea or the Gulf – unless indeed they were King Solomon's, who went to Ophir, a place which may have been in India but has never been located with any certainty. It would have daunted the best of seamen to venture into an ocean where they did not know the landmarks – and to do it against the opposition of the Arabs, who knew them well and preferred to keep them secret. The first northerner known to have crossed the Indian Ocean was a freed Roman slave whose story is told by Pliny: in about the year A.D. 45, he was blown out to sea in an open boat by a storm in the mouth of the Red Sea. After fifteen days he landed in Ceylon, and six months later he successfully came back again. That led an enterprising Roman seaman called Hippalus, two or three years later, to work out or discover the secret of navigation in the Indian Ocean which the Arabs had known for centuries. This was the constant seasonal variation of the monsoon winds. Using these winds, as Arabs had always used them, Hippalus made a successful voyage from the Red Sea to India and back; and he was followed by other Romans during the remaining centuries of their empire.

Thus the Arabs were not the only seamen on the ancient trade route. Indians always used it, and Egyptians, Greeks and Romans used it in their turn. Chinese ships from time to time made the long journey to southern Arabia and even Babylon. But the Arabs were its constant factor from the earliest ages, and after the time of the Prophet, with the spread of Islam, they began to sail to the Spice Islands, Java and Sumatra, and to China itself. The adventures of Sinbad the Sailor, the most famous of Arab seamen, are a mixture of legends from many sources; but they are told in a framework of the true explorations of Arabian ships in the 8th to 10th centuries A.D.

•

What ships then did they use? The earliest picture of an Arab ship, so far as I know, was painted in Mesopotamia in A.D. 1237. It is a comic and fanciful picture with several mysterious features. But the ship is undeniably a boom. Here are the straight raking stem, the high stemhead, the rudder hung on the sternpost; the captain, who looks Persian, sits in state on the poop – all familiar sights in the Gulf today. Two sailors seem to be bailing with earthenware jars; and bailing, one must admit, is a frequent occupation in many Arab ships. Above them six merchants peer out, each from his own cabin which appears to be built on deck: modern booms have no cabin of any sort, but an early account suggests that when many merchants travelled together on a ship a separate cabin was built for each of them, not perhaps for his own privacy but as a lock-up for his stock-in-trade. I wish I could offer an explanation of the sails, but they are unlike anything I have ever seen or imagined.

Booms without doubt have been in constant use ever since that picture was painted, and it seems to me probable that their ancestors back to Sumerian times were much the same in design. They may have been smaller, but they must have been big enough to stay at sea for months. Here we have a period of nearly four thousand years, from say 2500 B.C. to A.D. 1200, in which the same trade route existed. At the beginning of it, we know that seagoing ships were in use; at the end of it, we find it used by the most primitive seagoing ships it is possible to conceive. What other ship could the boom have evolved from?

It has no possible ancestor, except a smaller boom. One cannot look for scientific proof that the boom has outlived almost every other human creation, but at least one must say it is likely; and when I sailed out of Bahrain in a boom in 1976, it pleased me to think that the same sort of ship had sailed out of that harbour before the Book of Genesis was written, and even – remembering the Sumerian story of the flood – that Noah's Ark may have been a Bahraini boom.

•

Between 1250 and 1500 several adventure stories were written by Persian and European merchants who travelled on these routes. But the writers were landsmen, and their accounts are annoyingly vague from a seaman's point of view. They described their sufferings in storms and their fears of shipwrecks, which were frequent; but they wrote very little about the ships they sailed in. In 1437, for instance, a Persian named Abd-er-Razzak embarked for India at the port of Ormuz, on an island at the southern end of the Gulf, where he met merchants from every country in the east between Egypt and China. He wrote nothing about the ship, but an eloquent account of being seasick: 'As soon as I caught the smell of the vessel, and all the terrors of the sea presented themselves before me, I fell into so deep a swoon that only my breathing showed I was still alive. The mirror of my understanding was covered with rust, and the hurricane of such painful circumstances extinguished the lamp of my mind, so that I fell into a state of apathetic stupidity.' He was so ill that he went ashore at Muscat to wait for calmer weather, and in a second attempt, with a favourable wind, he reached Calicut in India, a distance of some 1200 miles, in 18 days.

In about 1420 a Venetian called Nicolo di Conti set out from Baghdad by ship down the river Euphrates and sailed to China. He described one very advanced kind of ship. 'They build some much larger than ours, capable of carrying two thousand butts, with five sails and as many masts . . . Some ships are built in compartments, so that should one part be shattered, the other parts remaining intact may complete the voyage.' These seem to have been Indian rather than Arab dhows, but wherever they came from they were far ahead of their time: watertight compartments

الفرآن ثم وبعد اساطير بلادها وخارف جلادها وقال ازكبوافيها بسمرالله مجرّاها

ومرساها ثم نفس نفس المغرمين اوعبادالله لكرين وقال اما انا

An Arab or Persian ship, undeniably a boom,
from a Mesopotamian manuscript of 1237 A.D.

were not used in Europe until the 19th century.

Later, more nautical travellers were astonished by one peculiarity of the Arab ships. A Genoese, Hieronimo di San Stefano, noticed it in the second half of the 15th century when he sailed down the Red Sea on the way to Sumatra: 'We embarked on board a ship, the timbers of which were sewn together with cords and the sails made of rush mats.' This ship took no less than fifty days to progress down the Red Sea to Aden. There he transferred to another, 'with sails of cotton but also fastened with cords', and made Calicut in twenty-five days without sighting land.

Indeed it was true that dhows in the 15th century, even the largest, were built without any nails, and no doubt they always had been. Their planks were fastened to each other by neat stitches of cord made from palm fibres, threaded through holes. The stitches can be seen in the picture of 1237. Dhow-builders began to use iron nails when they saw them on European ships, and modern dhows are always fastened with nails. But the change was not made abruptly: changes in boatbuilding techniques are always slow. Sir Bartle Frere, who was a distinguished administrator of Queen Victoria's empire, said he had seen a dhow of 200 tons which was fastened with stitches, and that must have been in the middle of the 19th century. There are two model dhows in the National Maritime Museum at Greenwich which were made in this way in the 1890s by an old Arab shipwright who remembered how it was done. For smaller boats, stitching lasted until quite recent times, and is probably still in use in some remote places. I have never seen a stitched wooden boat, but the well-known sailor Alan Villiers saw them and photographed one in south-east Arabia in 1938.

In the picture of 1237 and the models of 1890, the stitches are in pairs, and in the models they are taken round small wooden battens laid along the inside of the seams between the planks. The boats and the models have no frames, but large sea-going dhows must certainly have had them, and probably the stitches were taken round the frames or threaded through holes in them; though Marco Polo, who had a low opinion of these ships, said trenails were used. These are wooden pegs which are still in use in Scandinavia – they are driven in when they are dry, and they hold very well when they swell under water.

Another early account says the pegs were made of some kind of bamboo.

The 15th-century travellers thought of all sorts of improbable reasons for this curious way of fastening the planking of a ship: that the Indian Ocean concealed magnetic rocks which played havoc with ships that were nailed, or that the water of the Indian Ocean had the property of dissolving iron, or that the timber the Arabs and Indians used would split if it were nailed. They also suggested that dhows were sewn, not nailed, in order to make them flexible; and it was a common belief in the north from Viking to Elizabethan times that a flexible ship was faster, and less liable to be damaged if it ran aground.

They do not seem to have hit on the likeliest explanation: that Arab shipwrights had plenty of palm fibre – it grew all round them – but the nearest iron mines were in India. They imported their teak from India, and no doubt they could have imported iron too; but it would have been more expensive, and why should they bother when the home-grown product worked all right? Boatbuilders all over the world are notorious for their conservative habits. Palm fibre was something the Arabs had known and used for thousands of years, they were adept at spinning it into ropes of every size, and they understood its strengths and weaknesses. So even when they were building the biggest dhows they could, they went on fastening them in the way they knew.

'It is a perilous business to voyage in these ships,' Marco Polo wrote, and modern sailors might feel precarious if they had to put to sea in ships that in effect were only tied together with string. But after all, it is not an outrageous way of building a ship. The Vikings nailed their planks together, but they stitched or lashed the planks to the frames of their ships; and for want of anything better, they used the supple small roots of trees, which must have been less satisfactory than a fibre cord. In Scandinavia and in England a few pre-Viking boats have been excavated, primitive but upwards of forty feet long, in which the planks themselves were stitched together with roots or twigs of yew. It was said the cords the Arabs used had to be inspected every season and often renewed, but in that respect they were not much worse than the iron nails they use today. Their teak may last a century, but I have been told on the best of authority that the nails they fasten it with sometimes rust away within three or four years. To put in new stitching would do no harm to the planks, but to drive out old rusty nails and drive in new ones is a destructive process. Perhaps in the course of time they will take to galvanized nails.

●

For thousands of years the old trade route had been remarkably peaceful: no rulers of empires had ever succeeded in sending warlike fleets to disrupt it, and the only human danger at sea came from pirates. But on May 20th 1498, Vasco da Gama reached Calicut in India, bringing European warfare and atrocity. Within the next century, Portuguese ships had penetrated the Red Sea and the Gulf, and the Dutch and then the English came after them – all three nations prepared to fight one another and anyone else who happened to get in their way. But they brought one benefit. For the first time, Arab shipowners and seamen saw ships that were conspicuously better than the boom, stronger, more seaworthy and, especially, more imposing in appearance. They began to want ships like those, built of their own materials in their own shipyards, and other kinds of dhows came into existence, the baggala, the sambuk and the shu'ai. They were modelled as closely as they could be on the foreign ships the Arab seamen saw, the 16th-century Portuguese caravels and 17th-century English and Dutch East Indiamen.

It is not surprising that some of them wanted a change. Perhaps it is more surprising that not all of them did so; some preferred and still prefer to build the ancient boom. But it is certainly very surprising that having made one change so long ago, they have never made another. Modern dhows are still essentially the same. So they are like a live museum of nautical history; and watching them going about their work, one can still see the kind of ships that were used by medieval kings of England, or the kind Columbus knew, or the kind that made vast voyages under the Stuart kings in search of pepper.

Eight sorts of Dhows

The Arabic names of different sorts of dhows have always been confusing in English. The Arabs themselves pronounce them different ways in different dialects, and it seems to me they also use them vaguely: what is called a shu'ai in one port may be called a sambuk in another, and the same word may be used for two dhows that are obviously not the same. The confusion is increased in English because writers have to try to spell the dialect names they hear, and the spellings and dialects vary so much that the names become hard to recognize: is a zarook, for example, the same thing as a garookuh? I have done my best to sort these puzzles out, but I cannot hope that what I write will be the last word on the subject.

The Boom

Boom at least is a specific name for a specific kind of ship, except that some English writers have spelled it bum. I have already mentioned the primitive shape of the boom, and it may have seemed familiar to connoisseurs of old English ships. A boom is extraordinarily like the medieval Hanseatic cog, which was the seagoing ship of England in the 13th and 14th centuries. Here again in the cog one sees the straight raking stem and sternpost, the rudder hung on the sternpost, the deck set low in the ship, and even the high extension of the stemhead. Bjorn Landstrom's reconstruction of a cog is based on the pictures

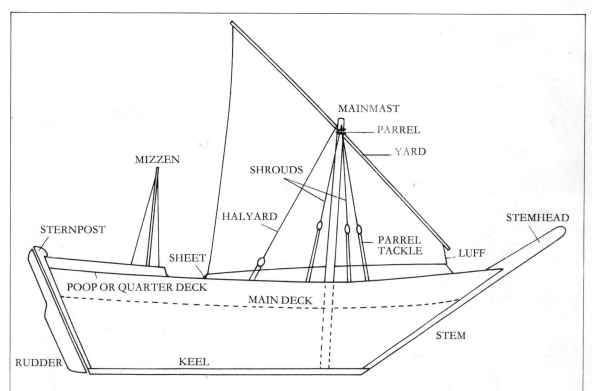

Parts of a boom. Few dhows now carry a mizzen mast; when they did, it was rigged exactly like the mainmast. The rigging is the same for every kind of dhow. Two shrouds are shown here, because there are two each side; but under sail, all four are brought across to the windward side.

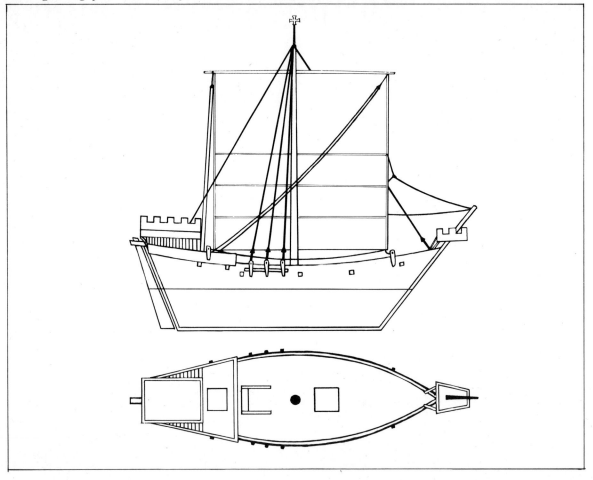

on medieval seals: if you remove from it the fore- and after-castles (a creation of northern chivalry) and the square rig, you are practically left with a picture of a small modern boom. There is only one notable difference: the cog was clinker-built, that is, with overlapping planks. This was the only method of planking that northern shipwrights discovered before the 15th century, but it was seldom if ever used in more southerly seas.

I do not suggest there is any historical connection between the boom and the cog: it is most unlikely that anyone who built a cog had ever seen a boom, or vice versa. It is merely, I think, that early shipwrights, in two places far from each other, were faced with the same problem and solved it in the same way. The problem was to carry bulky cargoes, and it arose much earlier on the eastern trade route than it did in northern Europe; the solution was to build a ship that was broad in the beam and deep; and the key to it was to give up the idea of rowing. As soon as the bold decision was made to do without oars, a ship

could be built much higher and deeper and more capacious, and the cog and the boom were the logical, simple and immediate result. The cog was the first northern ship that could not be rowed but relied entirely on sail; it did not evolve from anything before it, and was totally different from its predecessors, the ships of Viking type. I think each of these similar ships, the boom and the cog, represents the first great jump from a rowing-and-sailing ship to a purely sailing cargo-carrier; but the boom, which probably made the jump long ages before the cog, has lasted ever since.

There was another novelty about the cog in its day: it was the first northern ship to have a central rudder, instead of the steering oar hung on the starboard side of Viking ships. This epochal invention, a great improvement in sailing ability, was another logical step: once you have a straight sternpost, that is the obvious and easiest place to hang the rudder; but again there is not much doubt it happened on booms long before

Boom under sail

Boom ashore

Stemhead and aeroplane

it was thought of in northern waters.

Probably a cog was steered by a tiller, but the big booms have evolved a wonderfully cumbersome steering gear. The rudder has a yoke across the head of it, a spar which may be twenty feet long and is always painted with bands of black and white. On each end of the yoke is a small iron block, and a steering chain, with this two-to-one purchase, leads to a wooden drum on the axis of a steering wheel. No doubt this gear was once used with a rope instead of a chain; and nowadays this is the only chain in the ship, for even the biggest booms use coir or manilla cables for their anchors.

It is strange that the cog and the modern boom, so far apart in space and time, should have identical conspicuous extensions of their stemheads. On the boom, it is perfectly useless, a mere decoration like a phallic figurehead. But on the cog, it had a use: the cog was square-rigged, and the extended stemhead provided a fastening for the forestay. With a lateen sail – or at least with the Arab one – you cannot use a forestay. But possibly the high stemhead is older than the lateen sail, which itself is very old indeed; it may have grown where it is for a forestay fitting, indicating that booms were square-rigged in some distant age. The construction of it suggests that this is true. It is built up of five or seven baulks of wood, only one of which is the end of the stem itself. So it is thin athwartships and very wide and strong in the fore-and-aft direction, which is what it would need to be to carry the strain of a forestay. The stemheads of the other Arab dhows are built up in the same way, but none is quite so aggressive and spectacular as the boom's.

The rounded tip of this curious adornment is always painted black with a white line below it. There are only three other bits of paintwork on a boom, each with its own conventional pattern – the rudder yoke, the flagstaff and the sanitary box hung over the stern. Right on top of the stemhead there is often a small additional flagstaff, and often on top of that a carved wooden airplane. They say the fashion for this charming, incongruous ornament dates back to the first Imperial Airways service to the Far East, which was run by flying-boats and had a staging post at Kuwait. The models are still very fat like flying-boats, but now they have wheels.

We were lucky on our photographic trip that the largest, most elegant boom I have ever seen was moored in the creek at Dubai exactly opposite the Intercontinental, which is the largest, most elegant hotel; so the detailed pictures on these pages were taken in comfort on board it. It was almost brand new, about 200 feet in length and built on the other side of the Gulf in Persia; and it was in Dubai to have something done to its Japanese diesel engine. It had no sail, but it was built exactly as booms have always been built. The captain planned two voyages that year, one down the Indian coast for teak and another down the coast of Africa to Zanzibar for whatever cargoes he could find – the same plan a Dilmun captain might have made, except that dhows, before engines, made only one distant voyage a year.

This impressive ship had a crew of twenty-five and was bound for a six-months' voyage, and she had no human accommodation whatever. A dhow never has: no cabin, no bunks except a shelf for the captain, no shelter except an awning over the poop, no table, no chair for anyone but the helmsman, no sanitation except the open box with a hole in the bottom suspended over the stern. There is a space under the poop deck, but it is a store not a cabin, and is seldom high enough to stand in: on the Red Sea, where passengers are more often carried, I believe the women are stowed in there. Everyone else, captain and all, lives, prays, sleeps, cooks and eats on the open deck, or on top of the cargo when the ship is laden. The fresh water is in tanks on deck: they dip it out with a ladle and drink from the ladle too. They wash themselves (very frequently, being Moslems) by lowering an old can over the side on a line. Each man has a sea-chest, stowed on the poop, and that is the whole of his private world: it contains hardly anything except his own trade goods which he hopes to sell at a profit during the voyage. Somebody, probably the captain, has a transistor radio, which always seems to my ill-educated ears to be tuned to prayers or religious readings. Even now, when all dhows have engines, very few have electric lights: they use candles, and an oil lamp over the compass, and perhaps they carry oil navigation lights, but I think they seldom use them.

Cooks

80-year-old boom

Booms

Baggala at Muscat

Shu'ai building

Paintwork on a sambuk

Belems

Old sambuk

Ganja

Ganja

Paintwork on a sambuk

Boom

The absolute lack of privacy and comfort seems to be more than tradition, it seems to be preference; perhaps it is the nautical counterpart of the comfortless desert life. Lawrence remarked that Bedouin 'live in heaps', and never expect or want to be alone; and sailors in dhows must be the same. To have no shelter surprises a northern sailor; but dhows are mostly at home for the short season of rains. When they are at sea, the skies are almost always clear, the nights are warm and the days extremely hot. The open deck is the pleasantest place to be; and crews of dhows are adept at curling up and instantly falling asleep wherever they are (they wake up equally quickly when there is work to do) or at propping themselves against a crate or a bulwark in attitudes of total relaxation that are sometimes unconsciously beautiful.

The Baggala

Baggala (or baghla) means a she-mule, so it makes an appropriate name for a cargo-carrying ship. But if it suggests a plain and awkward character it is misleading: the baggala was the most ornate of all the big Arabian dhows. I say it was, because I believe it is extinct. Before the second world war, Alan Villiers thought there were 'less than fifty' in existence. Now, the only one I know of is hauled ashore on a beach at Muscat, and nobody I have asked can tell me of one that is still afloat.

It was – the one at Muscat still is – as good a replica as the Arabs could make of a 17th-century East Indiaman, with a low bow and an upswept quarterdeck or poop. It had a massive square stern, elaborately carved and decorated in the 17th-century manner, and it even had five stern windows; but sometimes they were dummies, carved and painted, and they never, I suppose, gave light to an equally elegant 17th-century

Baggalas at Muscat in 1870

cabin, but only to the bosun's store beneath the poop; for the inside of these splendid ships was just as austere as the booms'. They also had quarter galleries to resemble those that extended the stern walk along the sides of a 17th-century ship; but these were entirely ornamental, carved out of solid lumps of teak in order to give the stern the authentic shape and fair it in to the lines of the hull.

The baggala was frankly an imitation, but it is rather sad that its last examples have been allowed to vanish – recently, but as completely as the ships it imitated. It showed at least that Arab owners and seamen three hundred years ago set a value on nautical style and ornament, like their European contemporaries. It has disappeared in favour of the plain old boom through no fault of its own, except being more expensive.

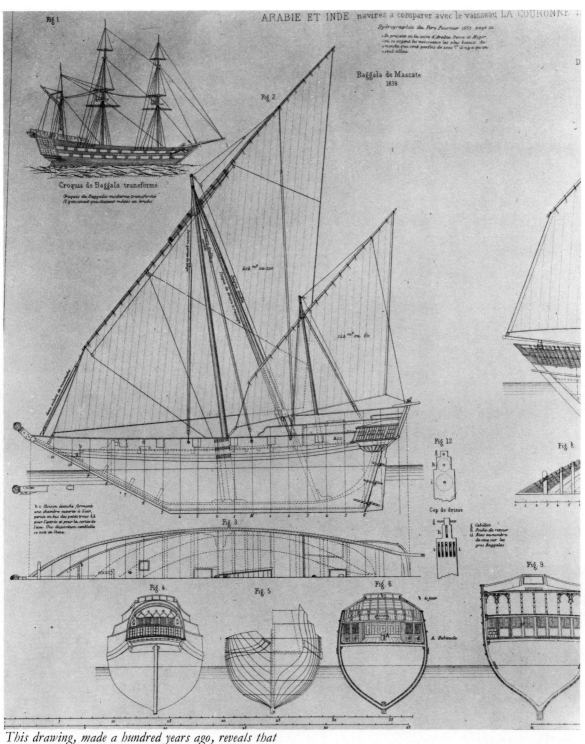

This drawing, made a hundred years ago, reveals that the lines of a baggala were exactly like those of a boom with the carved 17th-century stern added to it.

Sambuks (the accent is on the second syllable) are probably much the most numerous of the bigger dhows: they are the typical dhow of the Red Sea, although they are common also in the Gulf. To judge by their design, they are also the earliest products of European influence, the offspring of a happy union between the boom and the 16th-century caravel. At their best, they have the practical simplicity of the boom, and the weatherliness and grace of the caravel; and even when they are work-worn and dishevelled they have a family likeness to nobler ships, the late Elizabethan galleons.

The surviving pictures of caravels of Columbus's time are not very good, but they could easily be pictures of a sambuk. The stem is usually curved above the waterline, and the ship is low-built with a pleasing sheer that rises to a high quarter-deck with railings along its sides; there is a square stern, slightly raked, with an external rudder. The similarity is enhanced because both kinds of ships have lateen sails. But this is not a thing that the Arabs copied from the early Portuguese adventurers: on the contrary, the lateen was probably an Arab invention, as I shall explain in a later chapter, which reached Portugal from the eastern Mediterranean and enabled the Portuguese to sail to windward well enough to explore the African coasts and invade the Arabian seas.

As in the booms, there is one curious detail in the sambuks which has outlived its usefulness and become a decoration. Above the square stern of a caravel (and many other ships of the 16th and 17th centuries) the side planking was taken aft in a curve which supported an extension of the quarter-deck and sometimes a third mast. Sambuks still have these curved extensions, just the same shape as the 16th-century ships, but now they do not support anything, they simply stick out beyond the stern like a pair of trailing wings. They are even more conspicuous in the shu'ais, which are similar, smaller ships. They look so purposeful that I once asked a boat builder what they were for, thinking they must have a practical use, perhaps in fishing, that was new to me. He looked as if I had wounded his pride. 'They are not *for* anything,' my interpreter said, and he chose an unusual word: 'They are embellishment.' They do indeed embellish the graceful lines of both these kinds of dhows, and seeing them one cannot doubt they are vestiges of the 16th-century designs.

Sambuks have none of the complex carving of the baggala, but some of them are more lavishly painted than any other dhow. Paint seems to be a

Pearling sambuk under sail

matter of local fashion; the farther west you go round the coasts of Arabia, the more paint you see on the ships. In the Gulf they use hardly any, only the little patterns on the flagstaffs, stems and rudder yokes. Sambuks in the south have a band of decoration on their poops, but up at the top of the Red Sea they are half-covered with rough, elaborate paintwork in primary colours. Among their conventional patterns is an arrangement of ovals, diamonds and arches with a distinctly Elizabethan air; and sometimes on their stem or stern they have an oculus, the stylized magic eye which is the most widespread and ancient symbol in the sailor's art. Beautifully though they build their ships, Arabs seem to slap on the paint with a carefree hand, and for myself I prefer the rich

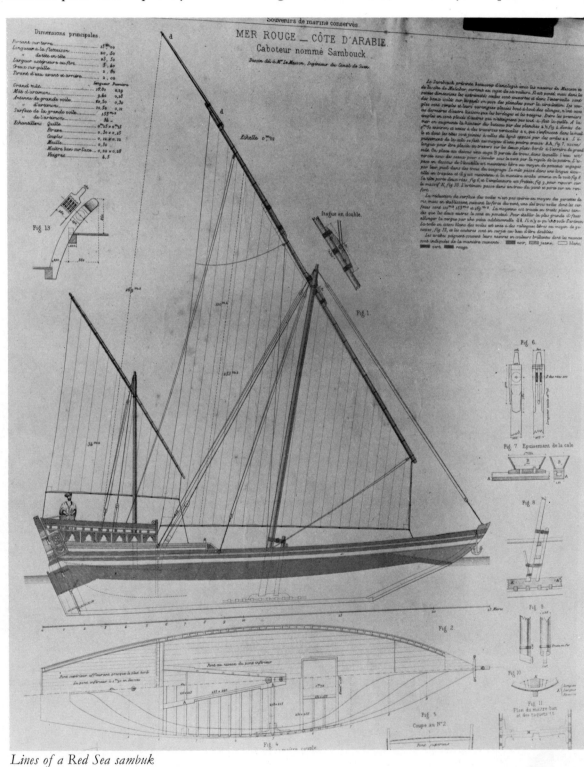

Lines of a Red Sea sambuk

brown gleam of their oiled teak.

Sambuks are built to the same design in any size that takes the owner's fancy, but they are never as big as the bigger booms and seldom as much as a hundred feet in length. Like the booms, they are traders and cargo-carriers, but for centuries past, at the time of the pilgrimage, they have carried people across the Red Sea towards the Holy Cities. Nowadays, there are easier ways for a pilgrim to make his journey, but sambuks may still be seen loaded to the last inch with human cargoes on their way across from Africa.

The smaller sambuks are almost exactly the same as the larger shu'ai.

'Wings' on the stern of a sambuk: apparently a relic of the 16th century

The Shu'ai

English writers have spelled this name as Say, Saiyah, Shewe or Shewee: two erudite Arabs wrote it down for me, one as shu'ai and the other as shuei. However one spells it, it represents (in my opinion) the most charming and elegant of all the Arab dhows.

An Arab expert will say the only difference between a sambuk and a shu'ai, as I shall choose to call it, is the shape of the stemhead: on a sambuk it is cut off in a single concave curve, and on a shu'ai it has a double curve. This is indeed a handy way to tell one from the other, but in my observation there are other distinctions too. On a sambuk, more often than not, the stem itself is curved, but on a shu'ai it is always straight; and above all, the shu'ai is a smaller kind of ship. There are shu'ais fifty feet long, but those are big ones, and there are little ones of the same design that are not much bigger than a dinghy.

I do not think one can offer a direct European parentage for the shu'ai: it is probably only a variant of the sambuk. But nobody could doubt its ancient lineage: it is a miniature of a late 16th-century galleon, like a beautiful toy. The low bow, the delicate sheer, the upswept poop with a little railing round it – these all seem to fit the period between the excessive top-hamper of the early Tudor ships and the equally excessive baroque decoration of the Stuarts. Sir John Hawkins and Matthew Baker, who created the 'race-built' ships that outsailed the Spanish Armada, would not have despised a shu'ai: Sir Francis Drake would have liked the look of it. I shall be told this is over-romantic, because one cannot prove an historical family tree; but after all, it was within this period, within a generation of the Armada, that Arab seaman first saw ships from northern Europe, the English and Dutch East Indiamen; and for me the mere shape of the shu'ai is visible proof that somehow the influence of that classic age of shipbuilding filtered through to the village shipyards of Arabia.

At all events, the shu'ai – battered though it may be in its working life – is an exquisite little

Ship of the time of the Armada, ancestor of the shu'ai

ship. Its underwater lines are as satisfying as its profile. Many now have very powerful engines because they are used for trawling; and when they are going flat out they show a splendid symmetry of bow- and stern-wave. A shu'ai would make a very pretty motor-sailing yacht, with a ketch or schooner rig, or even its own lateen.

I especially fell in love with a new one, forty-six feet long, still standing where it was built on a sandy foreshore at Ras al Khaimar, right at the southern end of the Gulf. I asked the master boat-builder, whose name is Muhamed, whether he had plans of it, but I ought to have known: he had none, but had built it, like any dhow, entirely by eye. So with his permission I took off its lines,

A shu'ai carrying fish traps

'Wings' on a shu'ai, and the captain's bed

as well as I could with a minimum of equipment, in the tenuous hope that somebody rich might agree with me and build a yacht that was like it – or better still, ask Muhamed to build it for him.

Shu'ais sometimes carry cargo on coastal trips – I have seen one perilously loaded with two Land-Rovers – but they are mainly fishing boats. As they are so small, the wooden structure that carries an awning over the quarter-decks of dhows is very conspicuous: they also use it to carry hemispherical fish traps eight feet in diameter. On most dhows, this superstructure is a rough affair made of mangrove poles, but on some of the shu'ais it is more carefully built, as part of the ship. Its aftermost supports continue upwards the rake of the transom, so they project well over the stern; and across them, four or five feet above the poop deck, there may be a platform perhaps eight feet by two and a half, with an ornate little railing round it six or eight inches high. Sometimes a well-made ladder leads up to it. This strange-looking structure puzzled me, and I asked a man in Muhamed's boatyard what it was, thinking it might be something to do with the fishing gear; and he said it was the captain's bed. I wondered if he was pulling my leg, and asked someone else in another yard, and got the same answer. I still have an uneasy feeling this is a standing joke in Arab boatyards, a foolish answer to a foolish question. If not, this must be the most eccentric bed in existence – the captain sleeping high up beyond the stern of his ship with nothing but the little railing to stop him falling ignominiously into the wake beneath him. However, he might well be proud, taking his nap up there, to be captain of such a supremely elegant fishing boat.

Well laden

Shu'ai at full speed

The Ganja

A ganja is a large ship and seems to be identical with the Indian dhow called a khotia. One sees them fairly often in Arabia and some are certainly owned and captained by Arabs. But I doubt if they can really be called a kind of Arab dhow; probably they were all built in India and bought from Indian or Pakistani owners. Their main distinction is a figurehead which is certainly Indian in origin, a carved, stylized head of a bird looking backwards over its shoulder; and their main interest, since the extinction of the baggala, is that they have the 17th-century stern, shaped like a heraldic shield. It is sometimes carved, but never so finely as a baggala's; and sometimes, one must admit, it is only a rough, lop-sided bit of planking. But on the best of the ganjas one can still see that strangest of all the ancient relics, the carved dummy quarter galleries.

Stemhead of a ganja

Stern of a ganja: less ornate than the baggala

The Zarook

Properly speaking, a zarook is a large double-ended dhow, the equivalent in the Red Sea of the boom in the Gulf. It is more slender and looks a faster ship than a boom, and it has a curved stem and sternpost. It seems to me to be a hybrid in design, but this, rather than the boom itself, may be the ancient Red Sea ship which mated, so to speak, with the caravel to produce the sambuk. Its speed is said to have made it popular in the 19th century when the slave trade was still active and the British navy was endeavouring to stop it, and it is still to be seen in south-east Arabia; but now it is not so widespread or common as the sambuk or the boom.

Travellers in the early 19th century noticed a very peculiar rudder and steering gear on some zarooks, and this still exists on a smaller double-ended dhow on the coast of Muscat. To me, the name of this small boat is something of an enigma: some people call it a zarook and some a badan, and a French naval architect named Edmond Paris, who drew an identical boat in 1870, recorded it as

a garookuh. I have seen these boats, decrepit but still in use, in southern Arabia, and there is one which has been repainted in a museum at Dubai; and whatever they are properly called, they are such an oddity and so evidently ancient that they merit a description.

In profile, they are like a flattened-out boom, with the three-piece structure of keel, stem and sternpost carried to an ultimate conclusion. The stem is raked to an angle of seventy degrees, and extended into a long, projecting, cheerfully-painted snout, not unlike the ram of a medieval Mediterranean galley. The sternpost has become almost horizontal, and on the after end of it are four vertical planks which look like an outsized rudder but are not: they are fixed to the boat, not hinged, and the use of them is anybody's guess. The real rudder is a further extension, with a high ornamental peak on it; and this is not fixed to the boat at all, except by two loops of line. The lower loop is knotted through a hole in the sternpost; the other end of it goes through a hole in the

A kind of zarook popular in the 19th-century slave trade

Old zarook or badan on the coast of Oman

Bow and stern in the museum at Dubai

46

rudder and up to the gunwale, where it is made fast within reach of the helmsman's hand. The upper loop is diagonal, so that it slackens if the rudder lifts. The reason for all this is that the rudder is deeper than the boat, and therefore has to be unshipped in shallow water. The helmsman lets go his end of the lower line, and the whole rudder falls off and is towed astern. But there seems to be no possible way of putting it on again without jumping overboard.

There is a certain rather zany logic in this arrangement, but none in the steering gear. The rudder has a kind of tiller, but it sticks out astern, in the opposite direction to any other tiller. Two rudder lines are attached to it. But, evidently, they cannot have any leverage unless they are widely separated. To separate them, two little spars are pivoted on the sides of the boat, forward of where the helmsman sits. The rudder lines are attached to the outboard ends of these spars, and to the inboard ends two more lines which the helmsman holds in his hands like reins. None of this complication would be needed, of course, if the rudder had either a yoke (like a boom) or a tiller put on the right way round (like a shu'ai's or anyone else's); but this kind of boat has certainly been built the way it is since the time of Trafalgar, and for heaven knows how many centuries before.

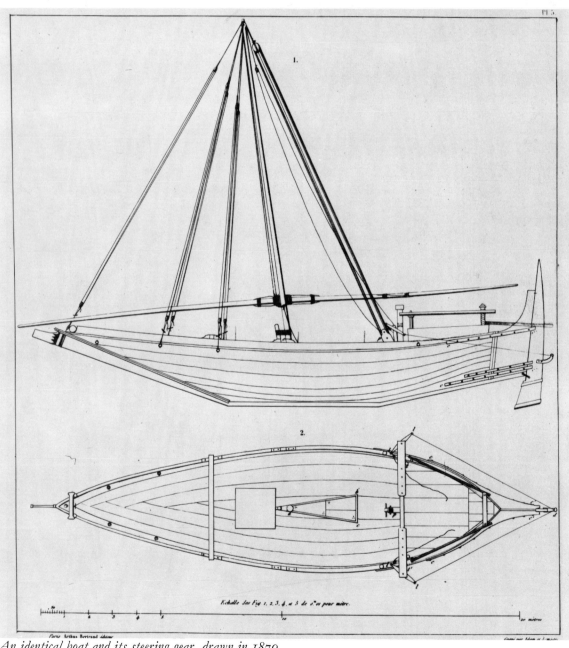

An identical boat and its steering gear, drawn in 1870

The Jaliboot

The word jaliboot, or jalbuti, is supposed to be derived from the naval jolly-boat. It is an attractive idea, and not unlikely to be true: Arab seamen have adopted many English nautical words. But the jaliboot has come a long way: a jolly-boat was usually the smallest boat carried by a Nelsonian man-of-war, but a jaliboot may be anything up to sixty feet long. There is indeed a resemblance: it has a straight vertical stem, like every small boat in the British navy. This distinguishes the jaliboot from every other dhow. To my eyes, it also makes it the only ugly dhow, a commonplace craft, tubby and stocky, with none of the rakish Arab flair – the sort of boat you might see anywhere in the world. Its uses, equipment and rig are the same as a small sambuk or a shu'ai; but I cannot imagine why anyone with a choice of dhows should build or buy a jaliboot.

Bow of a jaliboot

Big Boom at Dubai

The captain

The assistant cook

Steering gear

Parts of a boom

Pirate village, now at peace

Jaliboot on the foreshore

Jaliboot

'Wings' on a sambuk

Shu'ai

Sambuk

Small shu'ai

Shu'ai building at Ras al Khaimah
Small Sambuk careened

Stemhead of a ganja

The Belem

Belem may mean any small boat from a dugout canoe upwards. The one I want to mention is new; I have heard it called a belem, and perhaps it has not existed long enough to have a name of its own.

It is a small open fishing boat, solidly built of teak like all the dhows, but almost flat-bottomed and without a keel, except a centre-plank which is rather thicker than the rest; and it has a low transom designed to carry two outboard motors, a small one for use at the fishing grounds and a large one to take it back to harbour in a hurry. I am not sure if it ought to be included among the dhows. It is built in the dhow-building yards

A new kind of belem, designed especially for outboard motors

alongside the shu'ais and even in the shadows of booms, but its only outward mark of tradition is the stemhead. All dhows have motors now, but all the others remain the same old dhows, built in the same shapes as they have been for centuries past. This is the only new one, especially built for motors. It is the nearest you can get to a modern mass-produced speedboat, if you continue to use the traditional dhow-building methods and materials. So it may be a sign that another revolution in dhow design is coming, like the last revolution three hundred years ago.

'The nearest you can get to a modern speedboat'

The Master-Builders

Having been a professional boatbuilder long ago, I have wandered round many Arab boatyards with particular interest, and learned at least two lessons. The first is in manners. Sometimes, if I could not find an interpreter, I have been quite unable to explain what I was doing or why I was being so inquisitive. If anyone had walked into my boatyard and behaved like I did, we would have suspected he was a spy from a government department or a rival firm, and would have insisted on knowing what he wanted. But the Arab owners and their foremen and the workers, who nowadays are mostly Indian or Pakistani, were always courteous and cheerfully made me welcome, let me and my colleague photograph them and their workmanship, gave us cups of tea in their tea-breaks and even held the end of my tape when I measured and recorded what most boatbuilders would think were the secrets of their trade. I dare say they had a good laugh about me when I had gone, but who cares? I am grateful to them all.

The second lesson is in technique. Arab boatbuilders break most of the rules we think are sacred in the north. Yet they certainly produce strong, seaworthy and even beautiful boats; and if I write of their peculiar methods it is not in criticism, but in recognition that the way we do the job in British yards is not the only way, and perhaps not even the best way.

•

For at least forty years, people have said dhow-building is on the edge of extinction; and indeed it has been through bad times when many yards were empty and a shipwright had to be willing to travel hundreds of miles to look for a job. But at this moment it is flourishing, especially in the Gulf. Oil has brought an immensely increased population into the Gulf, and the demand for fish has increased in proportion; so the yards are busy building new fishing boats of every size, mostly shu'ais and the motor boats I have listed as belems, but sometimes with a big boom standing on the stocks among them. I fear this prosperous moment may not last, because steel trawlers are being brought from Japan and there is an obvious danger the Gulf may be overfished. However, Arabs are not given to worry about the future, and everything in Arabia is changing so quickly that nobody can guess what will happen next.

An Arab needs very little to start a boatyard. He lays his keels on a flat stretch of sand, which is limitless, and hangs up some mats of palm to keep the sun off, and sets to work. There is not much sign of deliberate order in an Arab yard, yet it is clean and uncluttered and smells pleasantly of teak. Perhaps the reason is that everything is sunbaked. The sawdust, bone dry, blends into the sand underfoot, the chips of teak blow away in the wind; there are none of those ugly corners, as there are in most British yards, where weeds grow or rubbish begins to rot, or old discarded ironwork rusts away. Nor is there any waste: everything is useful, and everything is used. The smallest scraps of wood are gathered up to boil the kettle for frequent cups of tea, or taken home for the cooking fires. It has an ephemeral, nomad air. One feels that if the new boats were taken away, the sand would blow over the place in a day or two and there would be nothing left but a virgin beach again.

Some dhows indeed are built all alone on a village foreshore, apparently by a do-it-yourself committee of villagers; but most are built in yards that have been established where they are for generations, perhaps for centuries. These also are in villages. They are unfenced and unguarded, as if there were no such people as vandals or thieves, or inquisitive strangers like me. Some of

the villages have suddenly sprouted into cities; but you may still see the boatyard, under its palm mats on its empty stretch of sand, surrounded by office blocks and grand hotels. I know two that have been cut off from the sea by enormous schemes of land reclamation; but their craftsmen go on with their jobs as if they did not care what was happening round them, and when they have finished a boat they drag it with prodigious labour across the new land to the water.

Most, if not all, of these well-established yards have electric power tools now; but thinking back, I do not remember seeing or hearing one in use. That is not to say the shipwrights never use them, I expect they do; but they certainly behave as if they despised them. In the yard at Ras al Khaimar there was a bandsaw standing idle in a shed; and outside it, two men were cutting a log into planks with a pit saw. I saw them begin and I saw them nearly finish, and it had taken them four days of concentrated skill and unimaginable labour in the heat. In another yard, a portable electric chipper was lying on the ground, while a man faired off

the planking of a new shu'ai with delicate, patient strokes of an adze. Again, every nail on a dhow has to have a hole bored for it, but I have never seen anyone use an electric drill: they use a bow-drill, muscle-powered. These are the tools they like: hammer, saw, adze, chisel, plane, bow-drill and caulking-iron – and these are all they need. So they can build a dhow of any size anywhere.

The timber for new dhows has always been imported in older dhows; nothing suitable grows in Arabia. The Sumerians thought the people of Dilmun grew boatbuilding timber which lasted exceptionally well in water, and perhaps it is possible some kind of teak grew then in that Garden of Eden; but it is more likely that even then they were bringing teak from India, and they have certainly done so since time immemorial. Nowadays, most of their planking comes in boards ready sawn and squared and stamped with their port of origin, Calicut or Kerala. Every established yard has also a stack of big squared logs for keels and stems, and an indiscriminate heap of crooks which they pick over to make

Shu'ai building

Sternpost and propeller aperture

Fitting of the first two runs of planking

Plank ends set into the stem

knee bolted on inside to stiffen it, but they seem to manage without one. The rake of the stem and sternpost, like everything else, is decided by what a Scottish builder would call the look o' the eye.

Next, the Arab shipwright starts forthwith to plank his ship; and here is a technical difference. The first plank (the garboard strake) is not nailed from the outside into a rebate on the keel, or into a keelson: it is set in a deep groove chiselled out of the keel, and nailed vertically down from the inside:

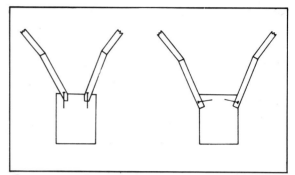

Cross section of Arab and British keels

The plank's ends are set into the stem in the same way, like the staves of a barrel, and if they are nailed at all the nail is driven down through the top edge of the plank. This method leaves the keel and stem standing out about three-quarters of an inch beyond the run of the planking, but that does not matter much; and probably on the whole the Arab way of doing this job is better and stronger, though more laborious. They use short temporary crooks, nailed on to the sides of the keel, to put the necessary twist into the first two planks.

Then they carry on planking: and this, to a northern builder, is the strangest difference of all. Making a carvel-built boat, we would saw the frames first and set them up – or at least, the majority of them – using drawings or moulds from a previous boat to get the shape of the frames; and then we would fasten the planks outside them. But an Arab contrives to plank the whole boat, and then makes frames to fit inside it. Here or there, where the planks will not lie together, and especially on the butts, he may put in a short piece of framing to hold them together, or he may nail on a temporary cross-piece on the outside.

In northern yards, a clinker-built boat is made this way, with the planks first and the frames

their frames and knees.

Teak is the best of all boatbuilding timbers, and so expensive in England nowadays that very few yachts are even decked with it, let alone built of it entirely. Burma teak is supposed to be better than the Indian teak the Arabs use, but the sight of so much of it lying around makes an English boatbuilder's mouth water. Even their scaffold planks are teak.

The first step, of course, in building any boat is to square off a log for the keel and lay it so that the waterline of the boat will be level. Most dhows have the same draught fore and aft, and therefore the keel itself is level: it is simply set down on wooden blocks in the sand. Then the stem and sternposts are set up. These on a dhow are tenoned into the keel, and the joint is strengthened by an iron plate nailed on each side. In the north, we would think this joint had to have a

A big log for a 150-foot boom

afterwards. In clinker-building, this is comparatively easy, because each plank is fastened on to the one below it. I guess that the Arab method dates back to the time when their planks were sewn together, so that they could – as in clinker-building – fasten each plank as they laid it. But to do it this way with carvel planks, which are not fastened to each other at all, seems to me a remarkable achievement, and I have sometimes wondered in a half-built dhow what stops the whole thing springing apart and falling to pieces.

Non-boatbuilders are often surprised that a boat built by eye will float on an even keel. In fact, that is no problem: it is easy enough to make it symmetrical, and the only apparatus you need is a spare plank and a plumb line, which no doubt the Arabs use. But I confess I am surprised that Arabs do not use moulds to determine the cross-sections of the boats they are building. It seems to me extremely difficult and very skilful (and quite unnecessary) to plank up a boat without

any frames or moulds inside it, and bring it out in the shape you want it to be. But that is what they do.

It is only too simple to say a thing is impossible because you do not know how to do it, but I suspect that in fact it is impossible to build a boat this way to exact dimensions. You never see a dhow that is obviously wrong or misshapen unless it is suffering from extreme old age. But they do vary widely in their proportions. The harbourmaster at Ras al Khaimar once read out to me the dimensions of shu'ais registered in his harbour, and I scribbled some of them down:

Length overall	Beam	Ratio length/beam
52'	15½'	3.35/1
52'	11'	4.73/1
41'	11'	3.73/1
32'	9'	3.55/1
23'	10'	2.30/1

I would have liked to know whether the variation of the ratio was entirely intentional, or partly a matter of chance; but that is a question you cannot ask a boatbuilder, however friendly. (Incidentally, I am glad to know that Arab boatbuilders use English feet and inches: metrication has not hit them yet. They also measure not only in feet but in arms, which seems logical: an arm is the length from wrist to elbow.)

But even if a dhow-builder cannot be certain exactly what beam he will end with, he has to be certain to give his boats a good cross-section, for their stability depends on it. They carry no permanent ballast, and ballast has always been useful to hide defects in design. An unladen dhow, especially a boom, is very high in the water. I doubt if they ever made long voyages under sail entirely empty; but they have to be stable, either when they are sitting on the water like a duck or when they are loaded to the gunwales; and this inherent stability, the way the Arabs do it, is created solely by the eye of the builder as he lays up his planking. That is the height of the boatbuilder's skill, a kind of instinct.

It was Samuel Pepys who complained that naval builders could never make two ships alike, and I think the same might be said of the Arabs, because of the very difficult method of building they use. But I would not have it otherwise. In England, since Pepys's time, we have divided the art and craft of boatbuilding, leaving the art to an architect and only the craft to the builder. In Arabia, the master builder is still the master artist, and one would not want to tie him down to exact dimensions. If you order a dhow, you may specify its length and agree its price, and ask for a good beamy boat or a slender fast one; beyond that, you ought to be content to leave it to the skill and reputation of the builder you have chosen.

The Arabs have one practice with their planking which would be thought a crime in a British yard. It is difficult to describe in words, and clearer perhaps in a photograph; but their planks are in two separate runs, the bottom planks up to the turn of the bilge, and then the topsides. In the north, all the planks are expected to run the whole length from stem to stern, which needs some forethought. But an Arab planks the bottom as far as

*Two separate runs of planking, and the gaps
filled in with short lengths*

he can go and then starts again, leaving a gap which is filled in afterwards by short tapered planks – some so short that they only cover three frames. One would have thought this was a weakness, and no British builder would be allowed to get away with it; but it is certainly easier, and seems to work all right.

By the time the men have finished planking, others may have begun to put in the lower parts of frames, but it is not until then that framing starts in earnest. In a big old dhow, the frames are massive and roughly squared, about eight inches by nine, and spaced with only four or five inches between them. There are several heavy stringers each side, but no ceiling or floor in the hold, and the cargo commonly lies straight on top of the frames. Grown crooks are used as far as possible, and alternate frames run across the keel and are bolted or spiked on to it.

In the smaller booms, sambuks and shu'ais – which are the great majority being built today – all the frames are crooked branches around six inches in diameter, and they are used complete. The men doing the framing choose them from the heap at the back of the yard, carry them on board and find the part of the boat where they are the nearest fit. Then they simply hew off the outer side with an adze until they are satisfied with the fit against the planking. I say simply, but this is obviously a highly skilled job, and I would have thought a dangerous one. If you make a bad shot with an adze, even with boots on, you are apt to hew off your toes, and these men, standing insecurely among the half-finished framing inside the ship, use their bare feet to hold down the log they are trimming. It makes my own toes hurt to watch them. They do not make much attempt to join the crooks together to form a continuous frame, but sometimes they taper and overlap the ends, so that with luck a couple of nails will go through the tapers and make a kind of scarph joint. The inboard sides of the frames are usually left in the round, as rough and knobby as they grew; and when the framing is finished and before the tops of the frames are cut off, they stick up above the planking as varied as trees in a forest.

Frames of a very large boom

Fitting frames with an adze: skilled and dangerous-looking

The nails that fasten the planks to the frames nowadays are hand-made, not usually in the yard itself but in the village smithy; so is the rest of the ironwork, such as the rudder pintles and even the anchors. The nails are very long and thin: they are driven right through the plank and the frame and about two inches beyond, and then the extra two inches are turned down on the inside. To drive a nail like that, a hole has to be bored for it, with the hand-operated bow-drill – probably ten thousand holes eight inches deep in a fair sized dhow. I do not know why they take the trouble: a galvanized boat-nail driven into the teak would hold just as well and last a great deal longer. The heads of the nails are very large and are not countersunk very far. Some builders put a strand of caulking cotton round them and others cover them with a kind of putty; but it soon wears off, and the great rusty heads are a blemish on the beautiful surface of the teak. To my mind, the nails are the worst shortcomings of a dhow.

Making nails and an anchor

Finally, the tapering gaps in the planking are filled up, and an old man who has a delicate hand with an adze goes over the hull, fairing it off in paper-thin slices. The seams are caulked with cotton and the timber is treated with oil – traditionally fish oil, but now, I think, something less smelly. It gives a wonderful depth of colour and warmth to the wood.

In every dhow, one frame on each bow is left standing up above the gunwale. The tops are often carved, and a strong beam is fixed across them at gunwale level. These are the bitts for the anchor cable, and also the bollards for making fast the luff of the mainsail. The deck is laid and fastened and caulked without any exotic practices, just like any European working deck – except that it has very little camber, and sometimes none at all: but who needs a cambered deck where it only rains three inches in a year? Last of all, offcuts of teak from everything are used to embellish the ship with its delicate little railings.

Tapering gaps and adze work

Bow and stern in the museum at Dubai

Master boatbuilder

Boatyard

Author and foremen

Shu'ai on the stocks

Fairing planking

Squaring a keel

Bow-drill

Village foreshore

Caulking

Frames

Pit-saw

Paint with a carefree hand

Laying the deck

Shaping a sternpost

Fitting frames with an adze: skilled and dangerous-looking

Hills of Oman

Fisherman

I was afraid I might seem to be patronizing and critical in writing about dhow-builders. But I did not mean to be, and nobody could claim a right to be. All boatbuilders are stubbornly traditional, and if – as I think – the Arabs' traditional methods are more difficult than ours, one can only admire them more for overcoming the difficulties. Their methods certainly succeed. Dhows are not just fair-weather ships. Their seas are nearly always sunny and warm, but sometimes very rough; and they stand up to them. Nor are they pleasure-boats: they are built for a long, hard, tough working life. They are inherently simple, and perfectly fitted for their purpose.

There are none too many things left in the world which are products of pure craftsmanship and owe nothing to industrialization. But dhows are one of those things. What comes into the village boatyard is simply teakwood and iron, nothing else, and the hands of craftsmen make a ship of it. What is more, the master builders are individual artists. They do not slavishly build a ship to suit an architect's design. Within the limits of old conventions each ship is their own creation, formed in their own mind's eye, their own conception of what a ship should be; and this, I think, is an adequate definition of a work of art.

Engines, Sails and Rigging

Writing about dhow-building, I have not mentioned engines. It is not that I dislike them, as fanatic sailors do: sailing nowadays is only for fun, and I think it is no good being nostalgic about the days of sailing in trading ships. But installing engines is not part of the dhow-builder's trade. He may fit the engine bearers and bore the hole for the shaft; but the engine is put on board somewhere else, after the boat is launched, and of course it owes nothing to Arab craftsmanship. Dhow engines come from Britain, Sweden or Germany, and most of all, I think, from Japan. To be fair, it is engines that have given the dhows a new lease of life that nobody expected forty years ago. They have doubled their trading capacity and made them, at least for the moment, economic again. Their sails have almost all vanished, but if they had not turned to engines the dhows themselves would have vanished a generation ago, and so would the dhow-builder's art.

Nevertheless, I think the sails of dhows are more interesting than the engines that have made them obsolete; for their sails were unique, a particular kind of lateen, and they were the ancestors of every kind of fore-and-aft sail.

•

Lateen, like dhow itself, is a word based on a misunderstanding. Western Europeans first saw this kind of sail on ships from the eastern Mediterranean at the time of the crusades. They called it a latin sail; and the word reached the English as lateen because the English heard it from the French, and in French a sail is feminine: hence *une voile latine*. But the sail was not really latin. It had reached the Byzantine Empire from the south and might better have been called a Moslem sail, because it existed on all the coasts the Arabs conquered after the time of the Prophet.

The ancient Greeks and Romans did not have it, nor did the Egyptians, but it is believed to have been in use in the Arabian seas since at least the 4th century B.C.: and since it spread all over the Moslem shores, it seems likely it was spread by the early Moslem conquerors and had its origin in Arabia like the faith itself. A similar sort of sail was also found by the first European explorers among the islands of the South Pacific; but it is hard to imagine any connection between Arabia and Polynesia, so it must have had two separate inventors. Whoever these inventors were, the lateen was a momentous idea, for it was the earliest sail that enabled men to beat against the wind.

The essence of sailing against the wind is that the leading edge of the sail should be attached to something solid, the mast, a spar or a stay. A square sail, hung from a horizontal yard, can only be set at a limited angle to the wind before its leading edge is taken aback. But if the yard is tilted down towards the bows, the yard itself becomes the leading edge, and the sail can be set much closer. It is easy to picture an evolution from the square sail to the fore-and-aft sail of a gaff-rigged sloop:

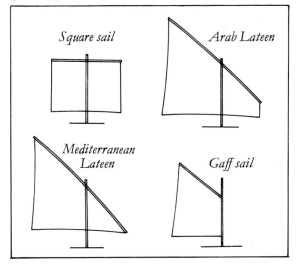

Square sail — Arab Lateen — Mediterranean Lateen — Gaff sail

Lateen sails of the Mediterranean type from a
Byzantine manuscript of ca. 880 A.D.

The Arab lateen

The Mediterranean lateen is a complete triangle, but the Arab lateen is not: its forward corner is cut off, leaving a short unsupported vertical edge which I suppose is properly called a luff. This has been taken to mean that the Arab sail is an intermediate stage in the evolution, as if the Arabs had tilted their yards that far and never gone any farther.

But I think that is wrong. Besides sailing to windward, the lateen has a second advantage over the square sail: it means you can set a much bigger sail on a mast of the same height, and the Arab luff makes the sail bigger still. Suppose the mast is 65 feet above the deck, which is a normal height for a big dhow: the forward part of the yard cannot be more than the effective height of the mast, because the whole yard has to be swung up vertically when the ship goes about. The after part has to be longer and heavier, so that the yard can be held in position by an upward force at the mast, and a downward force at the luff: altogether the yard would be about 120 feet long. But in a triangular sail, the forward end of the yard is supporting very little canvas; by cutting off that corner you can add several hundred square feet to the sail. The luff has a hefty rope in it and is held bar taut by the weight of the yard, so it makes an effective leading edge. A dhow can set over 7000 square feet of canvas in a single sail on a single 65-foot mast, much more than any other working rig that has ever been devised.

Most deep-sea dhows in the sailing days had two masts, a main and a mizzen. Some of them now have no mast at all, and very few have a mizzen, because the foot of it would get in the way of the propeller shaft. But some are still built to carry a sail on the mainmast, and it is a pleasure to see this archaic rig still created by living craftsmen. It is a splendidly massive piece of handiwork, made entirely of materials found on the ancient trade-route, teak wood and cotton from India and coir fibre from the coconuts of the Maldive Islands or southern Arabia. It needs no tools but the carpenter's adze and chisel and the sailmaker's needle and palm. The only bits of iron in it are the pins of the sheaves of the blocks, and even those, I think, are sometimes made of wood. All the ropework, by custom, used to be made on board by the crew on their long ocean voyages; but I must admit I have sometimes seen a manilla rope, or even a length of nylon, in the running rigging. Sails used to be made in all the villages where dhows were built, and even the cloth was woven in Bahrain; but I think this trade, if it is still practised at all, has gone to India.

The mast of a big dhow is a teak trunk about 18 inches in diameter, tapering only slightly, and about 75 feet from keel to head. It is stepped with a square tenon on a block on the keel, and it leans steeply forward against the main beam of the ship. On the forward side of the beam there is a post which is also stepped on the keel and projects five or six feet above the deck, and the mast and the top of the post are lashed together with a coir rope parcelled in canvas, so that the mast is clamped against the beam.

This mast looks as though it would stand by itself whatever happened, but it is given two shrouds each side which seem comparatively flimsy. They are made fast to any convenient part of the bulwarks and set up by tackles.

The enormous yard is also teak, and is made of four parts lashed together, a main spar with a strengthening piece (or fish) at the point where it is hoisted, and a shorter, thinner spar extending each end. It is held to the mast by a huge parrel – two loops of coir rope threaded through blocks of teak, which can be slackened or set up by a tackle which is made fast to the bulwark and rigged like the shrouds.

The most conspicuous part of it all is the halyard. The yard is hoisted by two ropes which pass over sheaves in the masthead to an enormous tackle on the after side. The only apparent reason for using two ropes is that a single coir rope that was strong enough would be very thick and would need a very large sheave. As it is, the blocks of the tackle, carved out of solid teak, are at least two feet square. In use, the lower end of the tackle is made fast well aft of the mast, so that it acts as a backstay – and incidentally gets in the way and causes complications when the ship is going about. The yard and sail of course are very heavy, and for getting the peak right up the leverage is very bad; and therefore the halyard tackle is sometimes rove with two falls so that the maximum number of men can find something to haul on.

•

Mast lashed to its supporting post

Mast, shrouds and halyard

The survival of this massive archaic equipment is not only due to the conservatism of seamen. It is simple, it is home-made, and it works: it has survived on these merits. When Arab seamen encountered the European ships in the 16th century they borrowed European ideas for their hulls – the nails and the square sterns – but they saw no good reason to make any change in their sails or rigging.

Both these separate worlds of seamen, in their past, had reached a stage when they wanted to set more canvas on their ships. They had both solved the problem, but solved it in different ways. The Arabs' answer was the lateen, set on two short masts. The European answer was to use topmasts and then topgallant masts, ever higher, and to set more and more of the old square sails one above another.

I will risk a generalization that I cannot prove: no race of seamen could have envolved the European-rigged ship unless it had access to forests of conifers – Norway spruce for choice, or possibly larch or pine. These trees alone provide long, straight, light and slender poles. Tropical trees, including teak, can grow straight and very tall, but their trunks are too thick for a mast in proportion to their height; and what is more, a tropical hardwood is nearly twice the weight per cubic foot of a temperate softwood. To hew a mast out of a teak tree is costly in labour and timber; and if it was anything like the height of a European rig it would be impossibly heavy and cause insoluble problems of staying and stability.

So the tall European rigs were confined to the temperate zone, and sub-tropical seamen had to use short masts. The Arabs could not have copied the European rig. But one cannot suppose they wanted to: their own was good enough in a following wind, and better when the wind was contrary. What happened in the 15th century was the opposite: western European seamen adopted the Arab rig, using its Mediterranean form; and ironically it was this that enabled them to begin to explore the oceans and invade the Arabian seas.

The lateen sail may have been used by the Phoenicians who sailed to England around the time of Christ; indeed, it may have been the lateen that made the Phoenicians the most successful seamen of their time. Its next appearance in northern waters was on the mizzen masts of

Mediterranean and Spanish carracks that traded to the north in the early 15th century. During that century, it was adopted as a mizzen sail in northern ships, and it was generally used in merchant ships and warships right up to the middle of the 18th century, when it was replaced by a gaff-rigged sail. On the mizzen, it was only an auxiliary to the square rig. But the Portuguese, the first explorers, developed the caravel, which carried two or three lateens and nothing else; and it was in these handy ships, backed up by carracks, that they beat up and down the coast of Africa and, in 1498, rounded the Cape of Good Hope and entered the seas the dhows had dominated.

•

The lateen never took the fancy of seamen as a mainsail farther north than Portugal; in the 18th century, when fore-and-aft rigs became common, they were all the lateen's descendants, gaff sails, spritsails and lugs. The probable reason was that a lateen is absurdly difficult to handle. Among northern ships, the one most reminiscent of a dhow is a Thames barge, with its one enormous spritsail. But a Thames barge can be and always has been handled by one man and a boy; a lateen of the same size needs a crew of nine.

On our photographic tour in 1976, I wanted to make a good pictorial record of the vanishing art of working these primitive sails, but it began to seem we had come too late. In 1960, when I was first in the Gulf, there was always a sail somewhere in sight; but now, equipped with cameras, we watched the horizons day after day and saw none. We were often told that nobody sailed any more: why should they when they had engines? Some captains said they still had a sail, and sometimes set it on a long voyage with a fair wind, to save their fuel or steady the ship in a beam sea. But all the time we were there, we only once saw a dhow which was sailing, so to speak, of its own volition. It was a large boom off the coast of Muscat, hull down on the southern horizon on a course for Africa. We hurried eagerly over half a mile of sand to the shore, and with his longest lens Robin Constable took photographs of it poised on top of the mirage.

However, we succeeded in the end, thanks to H. E. Tarek Almoayyed, who is Minister of Information in Bahrain and has a strong sense of his country's history. He offered to charter a big dhow for the purpose, and our colleague Khalifah Shaheen, who runs a film studio in Bahrain, succeeded in finding a boom which not only had a sail but also a captain and crew who were able

and willing to hoist it.

The ship was called *Najeeb*, 163 feet in length and some 35 in beam – a big sailing ship by anyone's standards. Her captain was Ahmed Muhamed al Naimi. We had a rather exciting start motoring out of the crowded harbour at Bahrain, because the steering gear jammed to starboard and the only means for the captain or helmsman to give his orders to the engine room was to shout to a man in the waist of the ship, who then shouted down through the hatch. (Although these large dhows have modern engines, they seldom have an engine room telegraph or a remote control.) At the important moment, the man who should have relayed the orders was doing something else, and the ship was going full ahead in a circle which was going to end head on against a merchantman at the quay.

Perhaps it is not fair to mention this episode. The best of ships is sometimes headed for disaster, and the test of a crew is in avoiding it. Everyone reacted with common sense. The helmsman left the wheel, climbed out over the stern and untangled the steering chain. Several people bellowed down the hatch, and the engine was stopped in time. The captain stood in dignity on the poop while they sorted things out.

In my experience, Arab captains are always dignified men. It cannot be easy to maintain an air of aloofness and authority in a ship which has no private quarters, or indeed any living quarters at all; but they succeed. Waking or sleeping, eating or praying, the captain is never secluded from his crew, but he is unmistakably in command. The crew may dress in any kind of rags, but he wears a white Arabian robe and headcloth which, in harbour at least, are always immaculate.

Al Naimi said he was round about seventy. For twenty-five years he had been a pearling captain, and he had only taken to deep-sea work in the 1960s. His ship *Najeeb* was only seven years old, built in India because it was cheaper there, but built to the archaic Arab design. She had a 240 h.p. Gardner diesel, made in Scotland, which he told me had run five years without an overhaul. He traded on the ancient route from the Gulf to Bombay and ports to the south of India, and his basic cargoes were also ancient: in Bahrain he had been unloading a cargo of Indian timber and lentils. Indeed, there were still several tons of lentils in the after hold, and before we set sail the crew carried them all forward and stowed them on deck, because the captain did not want to be photographed down by the stern.

She was built for that kind of mixed cargo. There were holds fore and aft of the engine for the goods in sacks and bales, but the timber was carried on deck. So her deck was placed very low, with massive bulwarks seven feet high, and when one stood on the poop she looked like a huge open boat. When she was laden, the deck was below the waterline, so it could not drain overboard and any rain or spray that fell on it ran down into the bilges and had to be bailed out again. In normal weather, this does not matter much, but it is a potential weakness. A heavily laden boom in some conditions of sea is quite capable of rolling gunwales under, and then bailing may suddenly become a matter of life or death. As usual, the crew slept and worked the ship on top of the cargo. The poop was the only space that was permanently clear, and here were the bare necessities of life. On most dhows the poop is open, with only an awning over it, but the *Najeeb* had a wheelhouse: it looked like an afterthought, a rather ramshackle structure with none of the quality of the rest of the ship, and it was unexpectedly decorated inside with pin-ups which were all the same, of a lady hippopotamus dressed in a ballet skirt. On the starboard side of it was the usual kind of galley, in a box like a large packing case; on the roof, the crew's bedding in bundles, and hung over the stern the two open squatting-places. Most of the rest of the poop was taken up by the crew's and captain's sea-chests; and here fifteen men existed on their six-month voyage.

Al Naimi sat on a box outside the wheelhouse to con the *Najeeb* through the anchorage off Bahrain, where sixty ships were waiting for a berth. He used binoculars all the time, and I had the impression his eyesight was failing him. He seldom spoke to the helmsman, but gave his orders with delicate gestures of his right hand, and he answered my questions with grave solemnity – but sometimes a twinkle in his eye. On his methods of navigation, he quite properly would not be drawn. 'There is the compass,' he said: it was the cut-off top of an old ship's binnacle. 'And the lead'; this indeed was huge, on a heavy red nylon line marked off in fathoms. He had some charts, but seldom needed to use them. 'I keep my eye on the sun,' he said with one of his twinkles. That was all he really needed for his voyage of 1500 miles to Bombay: compass and lead, and first and foremost a general sense of direction from the sun and stars. I observed that most of his crew were Indians. 'We Arabs are not seamen any more,' he said; but I could not tell if he regretted it. The Bahraini who was interpreting for us added: 'Every young Arab now expects to set up his own business.' 'You are all too rich for this kind of life,' I suggested, and he agreed.

I am afraid it was all a sign of the times. The ship was Arabian, but built in India because that was cheaper; the crew were mostly Indians because the Arabs were too rich to want to sail. Al Naimi alone was a true representative of the four-thousand-year tradition: and he was 'round about seventy'.

•

The *Najeeb* was built for an engine, and so she had never had a mizzen mast. But the mainmast was stepped where mainmasts had always been, well forward. Al Naimi did not know the height of it, but afterwards I estimated it from photo-graphs as 60 feet above the gunwales. The yard was 120 feet long. She could not have done much good on the wind under sail alone, because her sail plan was hopelessly unbalanced without the mizzen. But at least she could use a fair breeze to help her engine, and so her one mast was completely rigged in the ancient manner. The only modern touch was that some of her running rigging was factory-made manilla rope instead of the coir that crews used to make on board. It probably ran more freely and was lighter to handle than the coarse old rope of the past.

The first process was to break out the sail, which was in a big hessian bag in the storage space below the poop deck, and stop it to the yard, which was resting on stanchions about ten feet above the deck. The crew climbed along it like monkeys to knot up the coir stops, and the captain himself made fast the peak of the sail. There was only a gentle sea-breeze blowing and the sail was left hanging loose; in more of a wind, it would have to be furled while the yard was hoisted, and by tradition palm fronds were used to tie it – when the yard was up, a good heave on the sheet would break the fronds and let the sail fall.

Hoisting and going about ↑ *1*   ↑   ↑

7 ↑ *8* ↓ *9* →

↑ 4   ↑ 5   6 ↑

← 10   ↑ 11   ↓ 12

Rigging of two Booms

Hoisting

Al Naimi

Hauling down the luff

Going about

The sails set

Hoisting

Going about

Next, the crew let go the lee shrouds, passed them over the yard and made them fast again on the weather side. And then the hoisting. The fall of the halyard tackle was led through a separate block on deck and given two turns round a capstan of antique design on the poop. I thought they were going to use the capstan to hoist the yard, but no; it was only used to hold what they had gained when they had to rest. The captain stood on the edge of the poop looking anxious, the helmsman stayed at the wheel, and one man held the luff of the sail right up in the bows. The rest of them manned the halyard.

I had read one or two descriptions and seen a few pictures of the process of hoisting these enormous yards. The Arabs used to do it with ritual songs and dances. When a dhow was leaving port, the crews of other dhows would come to help, and it was said that sixty men could man the falls and still take half an hour to get the yard to the masthead. I think they must have been enjoying the ceremony and making it last as long as they could. The *Najeeb*'s 120-foot spar was certainly as heavy as any, but her crew made it look much easier than I expected. They sweated and heaved and shouted in unison like anyone hauling on a rope: but ten of them – I think it was ten – got it up in about ten minutes, without making any song and dance about it.

It rose, a couple of yards at a time, with pauses for rest and noisy argument; and as it rose it tilted, because the fore end was held down by the man on the luff. The parrel creaked up to the masthead, the halyard was made fast, and three or four men ran forward to haul the luff down harder: the captain was up there too, hauling with them and apparently showing them how to make it fast to the beam across the bows. The sheet was hauled in and made fast to a post on the gunwale, and the ship was under way. It was an enormous sail of coarse cloth, unbleached and as rough as sacking, but it set beautifully in the light breeze, 7000 square feet of it, the yard bending gracefully under the weight and the peak of it over a hundred feet up above the deck against the cloudless sky.

It was hoisted with the wind on the quarter: the luff was fast to the weather bow and the sheet to the lee rail, and it filled like a squaresail. But after a while the captain, with one of his gestures to the helmsman, brought her up to the wind and set the sail close-hauled: the luff taken down to the lee bow, and the sheet brought right across the deck to the weather rail. In that position, the sail was even more elegant to my eyes, and I think to his. I tried to forget the Gardner diesel, which was still unromantically thudding away in neutral below the deck.

Then I asked him to go about. Hoisting a dhow's lateen needs strength, but going about needs skill and good timing: it is a fantastically complicated manoeuvre. The essence, of course, is to get the yard and the sail to the opposite side of the mast. But they cannot go round the after side because the halyard is in the way: they have to go round the forward side, and consequently the ship cannot tack, it has to wear – that is, to turn right round with the wind astern. In a good-sized dhow the operation requires at least nine men, not counting the captain, each with a different job at a different post, and in anything like a wind at least three of the posts would call for several strong men each.

Al Naimi certainly knew exactly how it could and should be done with seamanlike precision, and standing beside him on the poop I felt with sympathy that he was shamed and embarrassed – just as the captain of a yacht might be, at a grand regatta, when he fears his crew is going to make a mess of things. I do not think the crew of the *Najeeb* had changed tack together before: some of them knew what they were doing and some did not, and those who did not believed they knew better than those who did.

The first step was to slacken all four shrouds and the parrel tackle and shift them across to the other side of the ship. They could not be made fast at once because the sail was in the way, so five men had to stand there holding them. In moving all those five ropes at once, it was only too easy to get them tangled at the masthead, and that is what happened. As the five men changed position, trying to sort them out and gazing upwards, it looked rather like an old English maypole dance, but it sounded different: everyone was shouting instructions to everyone else, especially the helmsman, who leaned out of the wheelhouse window and bellowed what I have no doubt was good advice – everyone except the captain, who ran his ship without ever raising his voice. Suddenly it turned into a fight. An Indian, who had one of the tackles, lost his temper and

Stopping the sail to the yard

Hoisting

attacked another man with a murderous expression on his face, swinging the heavy block of the tackle on a yard of rope – a lethal weapon. Al Naimi did not seem to hurry, but he was there in a moment, confronting the angry man with his silent authority. There was no argument: the man subsided like a pricked balloon, and the captain put all five of them in their proper places.

All that time, the sail was drawing and the mast was unsupported, but it did not seem to matter: I think that massive spar would have stood by its own strength in a wind that blew the sail to rags. The helmsman resumed his turn down-wind. The man in the bow hauled down the luff of the sail and then bore down on the yard itself, until he brought it to the foot of the mast and the whole 120-foot spar was standing vertically. It was checked there by another man on the poop, who held a long line made fast to the peak of the yard (in fact, it was the red nylon log-line). At this moment, one understands why Arab masts are set leaning forward: if the mast was vertical, there would be trouble getting the lower end of the yard to go past it.

As the ship turned across the wind, the man with the sheet – a heavy coil of rope – had to sprint round the outside of everyone and everything and back down the other side of the ship before the sail took charge. In a strong wind or a rolling ship, this must be a very difficult moment. There is nothing to stop the sail blowing out over the bow (in fact it often does so), and very little to stop the yard falling in any direction. But it went well. The sail began to fill, the man with the sheet completed his run in time and got a turn round a post, the parrel lurched round the mast to leeward, the men with the shrouds made them fast and hauled them taut, the man with the log-line began to haul down the peak, and the man in the bow quickly made the luff fast before it rose. The yard quite gently sank to its working angle, and the ship was on the other tack.

Then we asked them to do it again, in the callous manner of photographers everywhere. I think they were quite glad to have another go. The second time, it went like clockwork.

•

It is a pity the Arab lateen is so monstrously difficult to handle. It is not only the father and mother of all fore-and-aft sails, but also, to my eyes, the most elegant. Almost every other kind of sail has a straight edge, and straightness is out of place in the lines of a ship. But a lateen yard always bends, so that the sail in every aspect shows harmonious curves.

Some of the difficulties could be avoided by modern gear: for example, the yard could be easily hoisted by a winch and a wire halyard. If the halyard was run down the fore side of the mast, the yard and sail could swing round the after side, the ship could turn into the wind and the shrouds would be less of a problem. In fact, there is no reason that I can see why the Arab rig itself should not be the other way round – back to front – with the mast leaning aft instead of forward, and the halyard on the fore side of it. It would make their lives easier and save a lot of time in a beat to windward.

But still, nothing could avoid that delicate, perilous moment in going about when the yard is standing straight up and down and has to be persuaded to fall the right way. So I do not expect to see a big Arab lateen on a modern sea-going yacht, beautiful though it would be. In fact, I scarcely expect to see one anywhere, ever again. Soon, the few sails that still remain on the big dhows will rot or tear beyond repair, and nobody will think it worth the expense to make new ones. The few old captains like al Naimi who cherish them will have to retire after a lifetime at sea, and then the great lateen will be gone for ever.

As a postcript to these notes on sail, here is a photograph of something probably unique: a modern dhow fully rigged with a topsail. It was taken in 1973 by Major John Stewart Smith from a fighter aircraft of the Abu Dhabi Defence Force, on patrol to check dhows at sea for signs of illegal immigrants, and the ship was on a course between Muscat and India. To judge by the shape of the stern, she might be either an Arab or an Indian ship.

Topsails were a rarity even forty years ago, before engines came into use. This kite-shaped sail is set on a topmast which looks like a mangrove pole, and as the pole is unstayed it must be strictly a fair-weather sail. It has a halyard but no sheets of its own, so the set of it must depend on

the set of the mainsail, and the two sails must have been hoisted and lowered together. Rigged as she is, the ship could not possibly go about – if she had to, both sails would have to be lowered; but that would not be much of a disadvantage in the Indian Ocean, where the wind may be steady for weeks at a time. The big bowsprit with an outhaul is also a temporary spar like the topmast, and indicates she could also set a flying jib. The very small mizzen mast is unusual, with its yard hoisted vertically like a gunter rig. Her captain, wherever he came from, must have been an individualist: he demonstrates all the possible variants of the simple lateen rig. I am grateful to John Stewart Smith for permission to use this extraordinary picture, and to Michael Brennan of Abu Dhabi for bringing it to my notice.

Pirates and Slaves

In the first chapter, I followed the history of dhows as far as the 16th century, when the Portuguese arrived in the Indian Ocean and the builders of dhows began to copy the European ships they saw. Dhows never changed after that until they started using engines; but it remains to bring the history up to date.

The route to India, from the 17th century onwards, was controlled by the British East India Company, which had its own powerful ships, and later by the British navy and Government of India. Arab dhows lost some of their trade to European ships, but continued to go about their business in peace.

But the African route, when this period began, was under the weaker control of the Portuguese. Many Portuguese towns were overwhelmed, before the end of the 16th century, either by Arabs or Turks who came by sea, or by the

Africans themselves. On the ruins of these settlements, Arabs rebuilt a colonial power they had possessed for centuries, and under the Amirs of Muscat it grew to an empire. Its centre was the island of Zanzibar. Here the dhows were not only traders, but also the imperial link between the African possessions and the fatherland in southern Arabia.

Dhows, of course, had always been a familiar sight to anyone who travelled in those seas, but people at home in Europe, and especially in England, only began to hear of them towards the end of the 18th century. That was the time when the British had won world-wide supremacy on the seas and determined, among their other ambitions, first on the suppression of piracy and then, a little later, on the suppression of the slave-trade at sea. Dhows ran foul of the British navy on both counts, as pirates and then as slavers.

British frigates and pirate dhows

Piracy, of course, had existed all over the world ever since men went to sea. It was a mixture, in varying proportions, of sport and robbery and cruel adventure, and the English in their past had been as good at it as anyone. Indeed, there were still English pirates around in the Indian Ocean with bases in Madagascar and Mauritius. It had been a special menace on the coast of India, but the East India Company had put an end to it there. In the Arabian Gulf, however, pirates in dhows were flourishing, and it was the pirates who first caused the British to take a naval interest in the Gulf. Nelson himself was among the earliest officers who made the cruise up the Gulf: that was in 1774 or 1775, when he was a midshipman.

Arab piracy, I suspect, had more of an element of sport than most. It was an extension to the sea of the ancient custom of raiding in the desert, which was almost the only excitement of desert life. Desert raids were not meant to cause much injury or damage, merely to round up a rival's herds and make off with them; and the people who suffered most were casual travellers who could not recoup their losses by raiding somebody else. The same kind of raiding at sea was more harmful, because there were more casual travellers. The British could not interfere with the Arabs' desert sport and did not want to try; but they thought it their duty and right to protect a peaceful traveller on the sea wherever he was.

The sea-raiders had their bases on either side of the narrow entrance to the Gulf – on the Arabian side at Ras al Khaimar, where I admired the shu'ai in the boatyard, and near the Persian side on the barren island of Qishm. Between these two strongholds, every dhow or ship of any kind that went in and out of the Gulf had to run the gauntlet, and the raiders made themselves so notorious that this part of Arabia was marked in English charts and atlases as the Pirate Coast.

There is not much information about the kind of dhows these pirates used. At that time, European observers seldom made any distinction between the different kinds, but referred to them all as dhows or baggalas (they often spelled it buggelows), or else by the general and supercilious expression 'native craft'. Contemporary pictures show them as zarooks, with painted decorations that are not seen nowadays – but that may only be part of the same vagueness. Some reports said the dhows were three-masted, with a main and mizzen and a third mast right in the stern, like the bonaventure which appeared on European ships in the 16th century. In a chase, they could probably also rig a bowsprit and a jib. They had to be faster than their quarries, the deep-sea baggalas and booms, and in fact they were so fast that the English frigates and brigs sent into the Gulf could seldom catch them. 'They would tax the powers of our fastest yachts in light winds,' a naval officer wrote; 'I have doubted of success when rushing after them at ten and a half miles an hour.'

Nor were they short of daring. Soon after Nelson's cruise, the British frigate *Viper* was lying at anchor off Bushire on the Persian side of the Gulf when some dhows from Ras al Khaimar sailed into harbour. They asked the East India Company's agent for some gunpowder, and he rashly requested the *Viper*'s captain to supply it. The dhow crews accepted it with thanks, and instantly loaded it into their guns and attacked the *Viper*, which lost half her crew dead or wounded before she could drive them off.

That naturally made the navy angry, but the government of Bombay did nothing about it; and indeed throughout this period the navy was even angrier with its own politicians, who feared to offend the Arabs by attacking the pirates – although it was Arabs who suffered most from the pirate raids. The only person in the last decades of the 18th century who took any action against them was the Amir of Muscat, who possessed a considerable navy of European ships. But in 1804 he himself was attacked and killed by pirates. The British Resident in Muscat, acting all by himself, then took command of the Amir's fleet and put to sea, and blockaded the island of Qishm in revenge. He forced the pirates to make a treaty and promise not to attack any British ships. But it made no difference. They went on doing exactly as they liked.

At last in 1809 the Government of Bombay bestirred itself and mounted an attack on Ras al Khaimar with two frigates, a regiment and a half of British infantry and a thousand Indian troops. Indian dhows were used as landing craft, and the troops first plundered and then burned the town, and with it sixty dhows, presumed to be pirates, which were lying in the harbour. Again the pirates made promises. But in a year or two they were as strong as ever, or stronger: they began to make forays out of the Gulf, took four ships on the Red Sea route to India and ventured far down the coast towards Bombay.

All this time the Bombay government had been paying a bounty to the Sheik of Qishm as a reward for putting down piracy, although in fact, whether they knew it or not, he was a leader of pirates himself. In 1818, the East India Company's sloop-of-war *Hope* was sent to Qishm to deliver the money, and she ran aground off the island. The captain and crew were seized and kept for some weeks in the pirate stronghold. But in the end the Sheik relented and let them go. They came back to Bombay with a curious story: that the Sheik, although he refused to speak anything but Arabic, was in fact an Englishman named Thomas Horton. He was said to have stolen sixty pounds when he was a boy in England, fled to Sweden and led a romantic life in Russia, where he kept an inn on the river Volga. From time to time he had had to flee again, from a succession of wives and accusations of murder, and there was no exact explanation of how he had come to be an Arab sheik. The story was never confirmed by anyone else. But the English in those days were enterprising people, and quite often turned up like this in unexpected places.

It had always been hopeless to try to make pacts with the pirates because there was no one man who could answer for them all; they gave their allegiance, such as it was, to half a dozen minor rulers who were often at war with each other. However, the Amirs of Muscat still claimed a nominal sovereignty over that part of Arabia; and in 1819 the Bombay government agreed with the Amir to make a joint attack. From India, the frigates *Liverpool*, 50 guns, and *Eden*, 26, were sent with several cruisers and 3000 troops; from Muscat, three ships and no less than 4000 Arabs. This devastating force fell upon Ras al Khaimar and thoroughly demolished it, and did much the same to Qishm and other creeks and villages along the Pirate Coast. What was more, they assembled the pirate rulers and made them agree to a truce among themselves.

It was not the most famous of victories, but this time it worked. The Pirate Coast was officially re-named the Trucial Coast, and the waters of the Gulf have been peaceful ever since. From time to time, Arab battles flared up along the western shores until the power of Saudi Arabia grew and put a stop to them. But at sea nobody, whether Arab, Persian, Turk or European, presumed to challenge the British presence by warlike expeditions, and the dhows continued their trading unmolested. Pax Britannica, whatever its merits elsewhere, was an undeniable benefit in the Gulf.

Attack on Ras al Khaimar in 1819: troops landed from Indian dhows

Relics of three ages in a pirate village:
tyres, dug-out and a cannon

The fight against dhows which were carrying slaves was a much more complex and long-drawn-out affair, a conflict of moral opinion vaguely expressed and often misunderstood which occupied successive squadrons of British frigates for nearly fifty years.

Middle eastern society had had a basis of slavery since the very beginning of history, and dhow captains on their voyages down the African coast had always been willing to pick up a cargo of slaves if it was offered to them: sometimes a whole ship-load of slaves, and more often a few among a general cargo. Slaves were one item of their normal merchandise.

The British view of slavery in that era derived from the cruelties of the transatlantic trade and the treatment of slaves in North and South America. Evidently, that was a very different thing from the ancient slavery of the East which, right or wrong, was controlled by religious law and custom. The British could hardly have made

distinctions of policy between one kind of slavery and another; but on the other hand, Arabs could hardly have seen the distinction between their age-old customs and the bonds of servitude they observed in British India.

Thus the battle the British waged against the dhows was only an offshoot of their main campaign, which was fought against the American, Spanish and Portuguese ships on the other side of Africa. Many British officers, chasing dhows among the creeks of East Africa, were caught between two extremes of opinion, and came to suspect they were attacking the wrong kind of slavery and attacking it in the wrong place. Nevertheless, they struggled on, driven by duty, suffering year after year not only from fevers and solitude but also from constant exasperation – exasperation with the Arabs, with the Admiralty which gave them impossible orders, with the slaves who seldom seemed glad to be rescued, with the dhows which could outrun the British ships, and most of all with the sheer impossible size of the task they were trying to do.

But in those days, the kind of Englishman who became a naval officer could look at almost anything in terms of sport, at least when he was writing about it, and in 1873 Captain Colomb of the frigate *Dryad* wrote this period piece on chasing a dhow he suspected of carrying slaves:

'Only one thing damped our ardour. The dhow had two masts, and no sail was yet set on the second, or smaller mast. Could it be after all that she was a legal trader? While we were in the midst of such speculations, down came the dhow's single sail, and she lay apparently awaiting our arrival. Everyone shut up their glasses in disgust. Either she was a legal trader, unwilling to give us trouble, or she was a slaver meanly surrendering, without giving us more than a moment's excitement. Who would go a-fishing salmon if the fish gave no "play"?

'But what was happening about the second mast? A sail was rising on it; and on the foremast, a second and larger sail was rising also. The dhow had changed her night for her day sail, and meant business after all.

'The old *Dryad* was now making some commotion in the water. Nine knots; nine and a half; ten. Keep it up, good ship, till we get the third boiler! We shall have steam in it in a quarter of an hour, and then we shall go!

'Presently we knew by the increased violence and rapidity of the strokes of the screw, that the third boiler was beginning to do its work.

' "What is she going?"

' "Ten and a half. Eleven. Eleven and a half." Now we *are* going. The foam was flying from our bows, and the old ship trembling with the excitement of the pursuit. That third boiler was a godsend; we were gaining on the chase.

'Soon we were nearly within range, and began to ply the flying dhow with shot and shell from the little gun forward. There was now every chance of cutting her off from the land, especially as the wind was falling lighter. Those in the dhow knew it, and we soon had evidence that the shells were not pleasant. The game was up for them, and down came her sails. There she lay, a ruined speculation: a disastrous adventure in smuggling.'*

On that particular occasion, Colomb was right in his guess that the dhow was carrying slaves: she had a cargo of 113 'plump, well-fed, healthy-looking negroes'. Accordingly, he took the crew and cargo on board his frigate and sank the dhow: its captain 'talked of his loss as one of those to which his business was occasionally liable, and which he would readily make up for next time'. He and his crew were put on another passing dhow, and said good-bye, so Colomb said, in the friendliest manner.

Yet even this sporting officer, and many others, knew their efforts were misdirected. The cruel part of the Arab slave-trade was far inland in Africa where the slaves were captured by professional hunters, and on their march in chains to the coast, and in the slave markets of Zanzibar and the coastal towns. By the time the slaves were in dhows on their way to Arabia, there was really nothing the British could do to improve their lot. Dhow captains, left to themselves, did not ill-treat the slaves they carried; the slaves were provided with food and simply left to look after themselves, as passengers in dhows had always been. Captain Colomb wrote: 'I speak of what I have seen and judge to be the average condition of things; and I want to draw in the reader's mind a distinction between that horror with which we are all so familiar in thought – the passage of the slaves across the Atlantic – and the passage of his fellow across the sea of Arabia.' The horrors of the Atlantic crossing were 'deliberately inflicted by the avarice and cruelty of the European or American trader. If the slave crossing the Indian Ocean suffers, it is from his master's lack of forethought, and his master may suffer with him.' The condition of a slave in an Arab dhow, he added, was better than that of an Irish peasant in his cabin.

The British Resident in the Gulf, who often saw the slaves at the end of their journey, was even more emphatic: 'The treatment is at no time either severe or cruel. During the sea voyage they are not bound, or kept under particular restraint. Rice, dates and fish in sufficient quantities form their food.'

With this fundamental dilemma, the officers had to act under orders from the Admiralty which were appropriate for the Atlantic battle but not for the fight against the humble dhows. Ships suspected of carrying slaves could be

* *From Slave-Catching in the Indian Ocean, by Captain P. H. Colomb, R.N., Longmans Green, 1873.*

Cape Museldom.
Drawn by James Morier Esq.

Published by Mess.rs Longman Hurst Rees Orme & Brown Paternoster Row May 1 1811.

searched at sea. When slaves were found, or fittings for stowing them, the ships – if they were seaworthy – had to be taken as prizes to the nearest judicial port, and the slaves to a place of safety. Arab captains who were carrying slaves were not breaking the law of their own country, and the British claimed no jurisdiction over them: they must be sent home in peace.

But from the neighbourhood of Zanzibar, the nearest judicial ports were Aden, Bombay and Simonstown in South Africa, each well over a thousand miles away. The English could never take the captured dhows so far: they wrote them all off as unseaworthy, and sank them. The captains and crews were put on other passing dhows. But for the slaves, what could the British offer? If they put them ashore in Africa, they would never find their way home but would either die or be captured and sold again. So the captains took them on board the frigates and fed them as best they could, and from time to time they delivered them to Aden, where they were housed in sheds on an island until they could be shipped

to Bombay. There, in a remote and foreign land from which they could never hope to return, they did the very lowest kinds of labour for a living. The British officers earned a bounty for each slave they liberated; but they knew very well that the liberty they gave them was hard to distinguish from slavery.

There were other frustrations too. The British made scarcely any headway until the 1850s, because they could no more catch the slaving dhows than they could catch the pirates. They did a little better when they began to use frigates with auxiliary steam engines. At $11\frac{1}{2}$ knots, they found they could just overhaul the fastest dhows, which were zarooks. Even then it was difficult. Coal in Zanzibar was precious, scarce and enormously expensive. The frigates cruised under sail, and only began to raise steam when a suspect dhow was sighted. It took hours to get the boilers going and one or two chases were all they could manage before they ran out of fuel; and if they chased a dhow that had no slaves on board it, the Admiralty expected the captain to pay for the coal

he had wasted.

Yet it was impossible to know which dhows were carrying slaves until the chase had begun. Then, some Arab captains gave themselves away by altering course and trying to escape. If they had a big cargo of slaves and saw a frigate gaining, they often turned for the coast and ran their ships ashore, let the slaves escape if they could, and then rounded them up again when the frigate had gone. Sometimes a British interception made things much worse for the slaves: one Arab crew pursued by a frigate was said to have killed the whole cargo and thrown the corpses overboard to lighten their ship and make a fractionally better speed. But sometimes, if an Arab captain had only a few slaves among a miscellaneous cargo, he would accept his capture, prepared to fight a battle of wits with the Englishmen; and in this, he could count on the help of the slaves themselves.

This was the hardest of all the trials the British had to put up with: that once the slaves were on board the dhows, they did not want to be rescued. Normally, in a dhow, some of the crew themselves were slaves, probably born to the life. These men were not dissatisfied, and could tell the newly-caught cargo, especially the girls, of the possible pleasures of life in Arabia, and warn them that the British were cannibals who only wanted to capture them for a feast. Accordingly, new slaves were dressed as members of the crew, girls disguised as wives and small boys hidden under the cargo, and all were willing to swear they were born in Arabia. Frigate captains, using inefficient interpreters, often knew they were being tricked, but could not prove it, and they gave up the argument and let the whole lot go.

The British navy in that era never doubted its right and duty to control the seas; but the officers who fought the battles with dhows came perilously near it. They knew the only possible way to stop the trade was to stop the slave-hunters in the interior of Africa. When the slaves were at sea in the dhows, it was too late to rescue them, and was probably a mistaken kindness. By trying, the officers knew that in Arab eyes they were behaving as pirates; and indeed it was hard to explain the difference when they condemned a dhow to be set on fire or sunk, and the British sailors, before they put a match to it, rifled it thoroughly and took whatever they fancied.

Yet the British conviction that any kind of slavery was wrong obliged them to struggle on, many to die, all to suffer malaria and dysentery, criticized by everyone and thanked by none. They never brought the traffic to a halt. More effective were the equally patient efforts of British political agents ashore: men like Sir John Kirk, Livingstone's doctor, who lived for no less than twenty-one years in Zanzibar with the sole aim of ending the slave trade and at last, in 1873, persuaded the Sultan himself to declare it illegal. But not even the Sultan could stop it. It slowly shrank when the whole of East Africa, for better or worse, had been colonized by European powers.

●

It was a pity the ancient dhows and their captains and crews should first have appeared in the minds of the British public as pirates and slavers: piracy and slavery, all through the ages, had been no more than a small part of their business, and neither activity, in its proper context, was as villainous as it was made to seem in England. But perhaps some good came out of those years of battle – apart from whatever good they did to the slaves or the pirates' victims. The British came to respect the Arabs as seamen, and to realise that the trade of dhows was indestructible. The Arabs, on the whole, came to value British control of the seas: it was a nuisance to dhows when they happened to be carrying slaves or attacking other dhows, but an aid and protection whenever they were not. Certainly, in their encounters at sea, both races rediscovered from time to time the odd affinity they have felt for each other ever since they met.

Navigation

Arabs have a reputation as navigators, but I think, with respect, that it may have grown rather beyond what they really deserve. It is true their geographers and astronomers were among the early scholars who first made scientific navigation a possibility. But there was always a time-lag of centuries, in Europe or anywhere else, between the work of scholars and its practical use by seamen. There were three reasons: first, the seamen were seldom scholars; second, the scholars were seldom seamen, and the instruments they devised worked well enough on shore but were too difficult to use in a rolling ship at sea; and third, it was always possible, and still is, to find one's way around the ocean without any scholarly methods at all. The Arabs' reputation certainly does not mean that their practical seamen use scientific methods of navigation. They do not, and I am sure they never did. They get on very well without them.

The most ancient aids to navigation are leads for sounding, which are mentioned by St. Paul, and books of sailing directions. This kind of book was called a periplus in the Mediterranean, and a rutter, from the French *routier,* in England; and it is something of a measure of the antiquity of sailing in the East that the earliest rutter known for the coast of England was written in the 14th century, while the earliest known for the Arabian seas was written at the very time that St. Paul was making his voyages, the 1st century A.D. It is called the Periplus of the Erythraean Sea, and its author was a Greek who lived in Egypt. It describes the ports and trades and people, and some of the navigational dangers, all down the old trade routes, the Red Sea, the Gulf, the coast of Africa, and the coast of India right round to the river Ganges: beyond which, it concludes, are regions 'which are either difficult of access because of their excessive winters and great cold, or else cannot be sought out because of some divine influence of the gods.'*

Naturally, this wonderful book becomes progressively vaguer the farther from home it goes, but in the nearer waters its advice is specific. The west side of the Red Sea is friendly enough and has good harbours; but on the Arabian side 'the country inland is peopled by rascally men speaking two languages, who live in villages and nomad camps, by whom those sailing off the middle course are plundered, and those surviving from shipwrecks are taken for slaves . . . Navigation is dangerous along this whole coast of Arabia, which is without harbours, with bad anchorages, foul, inaccessible because of breakers and rocks, and terrible in every way. Therefore we hold our course down the middle of the gulf and pass on as fast as possible . . . Beyond these places in a bay at the foot of the left side of this gulf, there is a place by the shore called Muza [Mocha], a market town established by law. And the whole place is crowded with Arab shipowners and seafaring men, and is busy with the affairs of commerce; for they carry on a trade with the far-side coast and with Barygaza, sending their own ships there.'

The far-side coast was Africa, and Barygaza was a major trading post in the Gulf of Cambay, just north of Bombay in India, some 1700 miles from Mocha. Describing that far-off haven, the author – who lived on tideless seas – gave an eloquent warning: 'Now the whole country of India has many rivers, and a very great ebb and flow of tides, increasing at the new moon and at the full moon for three days, and falling off in the intervening days. But about Barygaza it is much greater, so that the sea-bottom is suddenly seen, now parts of the dry land are sea, and now it is dry where ships were sailing just before; and the rivers, under the inrush of the flood tide, when the whole force of the sea is directed against them, are driven upwards against their natural current.

*These quotations are from the translation by Wilfred H. Schoff, pub. The Philadelphia Museums, ca. 1911.

Their compasses look like the relics of wrecks of Victorian ships

For this reason entrance and departure of vessels is very dangerous to those who are inexperienced or who come to this market-town for the first time. The incoming tide is irresistible, anchors cannot hold against it. Large ships caught by the force of it are turned broadside on, driven on to the shoals and wrecked; small boats are overturned; ships caught by the ebb among the channels are left on their sides, and if they are not held on an even keel by props, the flood comes upon them suddenly and under the first head of the current they are filled with water . . . If you attempt the entrance at the moment when the seas are still, on the instant there is borne to you at the mouth of the river, a noise like the cries of an army from afar; and very soon the sea comes rushing in over the shoals with a hoarse roar.'

The Periplus, in short, was a practical handbook; similar books are still written, and in a somewhat similar style. But it was intended for Roman citizens who were new to these seas. For deep-sea Arab captains, then as now, these were familiar waters and coasts they had known since they were boys, and they had no need to look things up in books.

The first novel invention in navigation, after the lead and the periplus, was the compass. It came into use in Europe, in the form of a needle floated on a straw in a bowl of water, in the 12th century. It is often supposed to have come from China via Arabia, and this is possible: by then, Chinese ships were trading to south Arabia, and Arabian ships to China. But there is no positive evidence of it, and Nicolo di Conti on his journey in 1420 observed that Indian seamen did not know of the compass, but 'set their courses and measured their distances from the elevation of the pole star'.

I should think the same is probably true of all the navigators of the Indian Ocean. In England, long after the compass was known, it was only used as a last resort in fog and on overcast nights when the stars were invisible. Arabs and Indians seldom suffered those misfortunes. Their skies are almost always clear at the times of year when they sail, and the stars are brilliant: the pole star, low towards the northern horizon, is an unfailing guide. They had good reason, for many centuries, to regard the compass as a new-fangled invention, not strictly necessary.

They also had another guide to direction, the steady monsoon winds. The Periplus was written very soon after Hippalus 'discovered' the seasonal nature of these winds, and so opened the Indian Ocean to other Romans. It explains how mariners on the long crossing from the Red Sea to India set their courses by the wind: 'those bound for Damirica [in the south of India] set their ship's head considerably off the wind; while those bound for Barygaza keep along shore for not more than three days, then hold the same course out to sea with a favourable wind, quite away from the land'. It also makes it clear that Arabs had been doing this long before the Romans discovered it.

Di Conti did not say how the Indians measured the elevation of the pole star, but here again they had an advantage over northern seamen. The elevation of a star is easier to judge when it is low. For example, I know the breadth of my hand at arm's length subtends just under ten degrees. If I observed the pole star a hand and a thumb above the horizon, I would know I was pretty near the latitude of Calicut – or, at two hands above it, somewhere off the Gulf of Cambay; and at those small angles the measurement would probably be as accurate as anyone could have taken before the sextant was invented in the 18th century. (It would help to know what correction to apply, according to the position of the pointers to the pole star, but that is an easy and very ancient formula.)

So the captains of dhows on their ocean voyages have always had every advantage in using the simplest arts and tricks of navigation. They need to be apprenticed on their trade routes, but they do not need to be scholars. And as a final simplification, their normal routes are always coastal voyages. Not that the ships are always in sight of land – they may still, like di Santo Stefano 400 years ago or like Hippalus 1800 years ago, set a straight course from Aden to Bombay and see nothing all the way – but the coast is always there, to port on that particular journey, and if it has not shown up when the captain reckons he has run his distance, he at least knows which way to turn.

The most epochal crossing of the Indian Ocean was a rare exception to the habit of coasting. When Vasco da Gama had rounded the Cape and found Madagascar, he met a celebrated Arab navigator called ibn Majid and contrived to get him on board; and this was the man who took the Portuguese across the ocean to Calicut in

India, an action he lived to regret. But that is not to say that ibn Majid was a scientific navigator: he was a man of experience in those seas and he knew things the Portuguese did not know – the set of currents, the behaviour of the wind, the colour of the sea, how much northing he must make to clear the dangers of Seychelles, how high in the sky the pole star should be before he ran east for Calicut. This is the kind of knowledge a dhow captain carries in his head today; but I doubt if many would willingly trust their judgement to make the crossing ibn Majid achieved.

The modern captains, in their ancient ships, use the old common-sense means of navigation that took men across the oceans long before the scholars turned to the subject. Nowadays, they have a compass and a lead-line, and most if not all of them have some British Admiralty charts. And that is all – no patent log, no better clock than a wrist-watch, no electronic gadgets. I have met one who told me he had a sextant; but he was captain of the biggest dhow I ever saw.

Of the three things they have, I expect they value the lead-line most: it is a comfort to any sailor to know when he is in soundings. The charts – since the captain knows his coasts by heart – are mainly useful for showing the characteristics of lighthouses, which are difficult to memorize. As for the compass, I do not think they would be much dismayed to sail without it. (Most of their compasses seem to be bought in Indian junk-shops, and look like the relics of wrecks of Victorian ships.) They know the courses to set for each leg of their timeless journeys, and if need be they can set them by the steady wind, maintain them by the sun, and check them at night by the pole star. They also know without a log – by looking over the side like any practised seaman – pretty well what speed they are making; and they have a good idea from the height of the pole star when they have gone far enough and ought to turn in for the coast if they cannot see it. Elizabethan sea-captains used to say all you needed to go round the world was the Three Ls – latitude, lead and look-out. Some English captains said the same, in spite of the scholars, in the 18th century. It is still true, provided you are not in a desperate hurry – and the captains of dhows are seldom in a hurry.

I do not mean it is easy to navigate this way, and it is not as safe as it might be. It needs self-confidence, built on a long apprenticeship, and confidence also in the mercy of God. But it is in keeping that the captains of dhows should prefer that skill and confidence, rather than a bookish schoolroom skill in navigation. I find it very pleasing in these days, when Arabia is full of high-pressure salesmen intent on selling the Arabs things they do not need, that nobody yet has persuaded the captains of dhows that they ought to have sextants, chronometers, patent logs, gyro compasses, radar, ship-to-shore telephones or echo sounders. Long may their independence last.

Trades and Cargoes

The ivory, gold, rare woods and precious stones imported to Sumeria no doubt were the most glamorous cargoes on the early trade routes of the dhows; no less exotic were King Solomon's apes and peacocks, the frankincense and myrrh of the New Testament, and the silks and scents and spices that came from the east to medieval Europe. The 1st-century Periplus describes the goods that were traded at each of the ports, and mentions an enormous variety: to pick out a few, there were tortoise-shell, glass, rhinoceros-horn, horses, copper and brass, tools and weapons, wine, coral, slaves, pearls, drugs, alabaster, all sorts of jewels, perfumes, ointments and spices – especially pepper and cinnamon – and singing boys and beautiful maidens as bribes for Indian kings. In the same period, a classified list of import duties for the Roman end of the routes adds tigers, panthers, leopards, lions and eunuchs.

But among the strange and precious goods were a few that were mundane: cloth and ready-made clothes – some specified as inferior – wheat, rice, dates, olive oil, blankets and 'honey from the reed called sacchari'. It is these more bulky and less romantic cargoes that make the living of most of the dhows today.

One cannot generalize, because a dhow is the tramp of the Indian Ocean and its captain will carry anything anywhere. But a staple on the southward journey has always been the dates of Arabia and Mesopotamia. Just as the size of an English medieval ship was measured by the number of tuns of Bordeaux wine she could carry, so the size of a dhow was measured by the number of packages of dates; and one can still see holds packed with these sticky bundles, each wrapped in palm-leaf matting and as heavy as a man can carry. Dhows may also be loaded with thousands of sacks of onions, lentils, beans, corn, rice, sugar, salt, tobacco – anything that is not too perishable for a long, hot passage; and the decks are stacked with the Indian teak or with mangrove poles from East African swamps, which are an essential part of traditional Arab buildings. Big dhows bring these things from afar to the major ports, and little dhows distribute them round the coast; for even now great stretches of the Arabian coast have no road inland, and great stretches also have such shallow seas that only the little dhows can reach them among the sandbanks or the coral reefs.

It is centuries since merchants made a habit of travelling in the dhows: they go by faster and more comfortable ways, and take their most precious cargoes with them. But the captain, as a rule, is a merchant himself. His ship is often chartered to carry somebody else's goods, but he also buys cargoes in the hope of selling them somewhere else at a profit. The dignified figure in white on the poop is not merely the ship's master, he is also a businessman and is probably rich. He spends much of his time in buying and selling ashore, and conferring in coffee-shops with other merchants, when he leaves the running of his ship to his mate. In a smaller way, the crewmen are businessmen too. They are not paid much, but they are encouraged to make their own guesses about the trends of markets and carry their own trade goods in their sea chests. This was the way the East India Company ran its ships, to everybody's profit. It goes without saying that the crews of dhows are enthusiastic smugglers.

No doubt there are also professional smugglers among the passengers who still prefer to travel in dhows: there used to be a little world of people who travelled perpetually, moving from one dhow to another and making a living by evading customs everywhere. But the main reasons for travelling by dhow are poverty and simplicity. There are passenger steamers now that call at all the major ports, not to mention aircraft; but dhows are cheaper, and also less formal and

alarming, for people who are poor and unsophisticated. If you travel by dhow, you can make your own bargain with the captain for the few square feet of deck you will get for yourself and your baggage; you can pay to eat the ship's food or you can take your own and make your own fire to cook it. Also, you can slip ashore more easily, avoiding formalities. Most passengers in dhows are there because they are poor and humble. But nowadays, I suppose, a good many of the passengers themselves are contraband, illegal migrants of one sort or another trying to smuggle themselves into countries where trade has boomed and there is work to be had and pay is good. In some of the oil states, practically all the manual labour is done by migrants from Pakistan and India, and it would be surprising if dhows do not help to land them there, with or without the proper bits of paper. It would be one of those minor illegalities that do good to somebody and seem to do nobody any harm.

At present, however, many of the big dhows are working in an unadventurous trade. In the creek at Dubai, for example, one may see upwards of a hundred of them loading and unloading, entirely by hand, an astonishing variety of cargoes. Walking along the creek one day in 1976, I began to make a list of the goods I could recognize. I gave it up before long, there were so many; but by then I had written down not only onions, dates, lentils, limes, garlic and tomatoes – things I more or less expected – but also a list of things as exotic in their way as the list of the ancient Periplus: refrigerators, mattresses, wheelbarrows, water closets, washing machines, air conditioners, freezers, roofing felt, tea, coconut biscuits, rugs, shoes (from Romania), motor cycles (from Japan), umbrellas, canned curried chicken and cars; not to mention teak, of course. I was astonished to see the way the dhows were laden: some with hundreds of new motor cycles casually lashed together on deck, some with tottering heaps of foam mattresses literally bulging over the gun-

wales and even stacked on top of the framework which is meant for an awning. It seemed to suggest an unreasonable faith that the weather on their voyages would be fine and calm. It was a dusty, noisy, cheerful, colourful and confusing scene: confusing because none of the goods whatever were local products, yet they were being loaded on to the dhows, not only off them.

In the confusion, I was absurdly slow to, recognize two things: first, that half the big dhows in port were not Arabian but Indian or Pakistani; and second, that those most fantastically laden were not setting off on their long traditional journeys. Outside the port, nearly a hundred merchant ships were lying at anchor and waiting for a deep-water berth; and most of the dhows were only ferrying cargoes between the ships and the shore, playing the ignominious role of lighters.

At present, this is happening in all the major ports of the oil countries – Kuwait, Bahrain, Abu Dhabi, Sharjah and Jeddah are other examples.

Well laden

ges in Dubai: a dusty, noisy, rful and confusing scene

Shu'ai trawling

The creek at Dubai

Laden booms

Masthead and halyard tackle

Shu'ai loaded

Mast, shrouds and halyard

Onions

Fishing Shu'ais

Each country is hectically building new docks, but in the meantime the goods they need or want to import are far in excess of their harbour capacity. Moreover, some of the mushroom cities have developed as trading centres where goods are not merely imported but transhipped. I do not understand why anyone should ship a cargo of Romanian shoes or Japanese motor cycles into a place like Dubai and then ship them out again; but there are many mysterious ways of making a profit. As a consequence, millions of tons of shipping are kept waiting offshore at prodigious expense, and the dhows have discovered a new though temporary way of earning their keep, carrying cargoes not for thousands of miles, but only for one or two. It seems a sad trade for a sea-going ship – any old barge could do it – but when merchants and contractors are desperate for the cargoes there is good money in it. And indeed the secret of the dhows' survival is opportunism, a readiness to do whatever job there is, however humble.

The most picturesque of all their ancient trades has practically disappeared within the last forty years. This is pearl diving. The warm, shallow waters down most of the western side of the Gulf are prolific oyster beds, and they have been worked for pearls not only through the whole of recorded history, but ever since the origins of Sumerian legend. In the Sumerian Epic of Gilgamesh, a pearl of Dilmun represented the secret of eternal life: it was given to Gilgamesh, a hero part man and part beast, but he dropped it in the sea and a serpent ate it – and mankind lost the secret. It is a symbol as old as the apple of Eve. Pearling in the Gulf, one might therefore say, is the oldest local trade in the world; and perhaps it was in prehistoric pearling that Bahrainis learned their seamanship and were able, in the time of Sumeria itself, to dominate the long sea-route to India.

The pearls of Bahrain are often mentioned in history. They were known to the Assyrians in 2000 B.C., to the Romans and Greeks, and all through the Middle Ages; and it was pearls that tempted the Portuguese to enter the Gulf and seize Bahrain in 1522. The first description of the methods of diving was written a thousand years ago, and it might as well be a description of the methods of the 1930s. Nothing had changed.

Pearling occupied thousands of the smaller dhows – sambuks, shu'ais and jaliboots – for four or five months in the summer of every year. In the 19th century, 1500 boats would go out from Bahrain alone, and uncounted others from Kuwait, Qatar and the coastal villages. It was a trade of romantic ceremony and long-established custom. Divers were a community apart from other men, with songs and rites and dances of their own. On the day when the start of the season was decreed they trooped to the boats with drums and cheers and joyful celebration, and all set sail together in a multitudinous fleet.

Yet it was a cruel, unhealthy, dangerous and unrewarding life. A big sambuk, say seventy feet in length, might carry thirty divers: each diver had a mate who handled his ropes, and each ship had its captain and crew and a number of small boys who did most of the dirty work – seventy men, perhaps, who lived on the deck of that boat for month after month before they came back to shore. They fed on fish, but not on oysters, which they threw away. Once in a while, another boat would bring them other provisions, and they found fresh water by diving for it with leather bottles – for it is one of the oddities of that coast that there are fresh-water springs at the bottom of the sea.

In both the 10th and the 20th centuries, men dived naked, or wearing a loin-cloth or sometimes an overall cotton garment as a protection against the stings of jellyfish, and their only equipment was a nose-clip. Each man's mate lashed a pole or an oar to the side of the ship, and from that he worked two ropes: one was weighted and the other carried a basket. The diver put his foot in a loop of the weighted rope and held the other: his mate let him down to the bottom, then drew up the weighted rope again. The diver gathered as many shells as he could while he held his breath, then tugged the second rope as a signal to haul him up. By this means, they fished at depths of up to sixty feet, diving again and again and collecting perhaps a dozen shells each time. In the colder weather outside the main diving season, it was said they spent a third of each day in the water, resting on deck when they were intolerably cold; but in high summer they could keep it up much longer.

It was the custom to open the shells in the morning, before the day's diving began, because they opened more easily after a night on deck. Perhaps the gamble of those morning sessions was some compensation for the rigorous life. If a diver found a pearl, he put it between his toes: his hands were busy. At the end, the captain collected them, wrapped them in cloths and stowed them in a chest on the poop. The boys threw the shells and oysters back in the sea, and the men went over the side again.

In the long run, of course, this kind of diving was very bad for the health of the men who did it, especially for their ears and eyes and lungs, and probably their hearts – though it seems it did not shorten their lives by much; there are still old divers living in Bahrain. But once they started the life, they were not allowed to stop. As often happens in traditional trades, the men who did the hardest work were the last to profit from it. The captains could make comfortable fortunes, so could the merchants who came out in boats from time to time or bargained for the pearls ashore at the end of the season. The divers normally ended the season in debt. It was one of the customs that captains should advance them money before the season began, to provide for their families while they were at sea. Captains made a practice of advancing more than they thought the divers would earn; and so the same divers, whether they wanted to or not, were obliged to work again for them in the following year, and indeed to live as divers, progressively further in debt, for the rest of their lives. Worst of all, the courts held that diving debts were heritable, so that when a diver died or fell ill or grew too old to work, his son could be forced to take his place.

Nobody, least of all the Bahrainis, need regret the end of this wicked trade. It was vastly profitable for everyone concerned except the divers and their mates, and it formed an important part of the national wealth; at one time, the governments of Bahrain and Saudi Arabia prohibited the use of diving apparatus, for fear that outsiders would enter the Gulf and rob the oyster beds. Yet the whole thing was built on the sufferings of men who were enslaved by debt.

What brought it to an end was largely the enlightened policy of the Amir of Bahrain in the 1930s. He insisted on reforming the laws and customs of pearling so that divers could no longer be tricked into debt, and therefore need only dive if they wanted to. The number of men who went to the oyster beds from Bahrain declined in the following years from roughly twenty thousand to two thousand, and the number of dhows from five hundred to less than one hundred. The reforms coincided with other influences. The depression of the 1930s hit the market for such luxuries, and the Japanese undermined it with cultured pearls. Finally, the states and the people along that shore of the Gulf found easier riches in oil. Sometimes old divers nostalgically sing their songs and even dance their dances; but who wants to be a naked diver when there is plenty of money ashore?

However, the oysters are still in the sea and so are the pearls, and recently there has been talk of reversing the old prohibition and mechanizing the trade. Whether dhows will play a part in that remains to be seen.

•

I have never made an ocean voyage in a dhow, and now I am too old and sybaritic to begin: so

I have only seen their crews in harbours and day-trips at sea, not when they have settled down to their ocean routine. Nor has any modern Arab seaman written about those voyages, so far as I know. But luckily one of the most observant and experienced nautical writers did it in the 1930s, the end of the age of sail. This was Alan Villiers, and the book he called *Sons of Sinbad* is a classic of seafaring stories. To fill this gap in my knowledge, I cannot do better than try to convey the general impression he has given me – and to recommend a reader of this book to read his too.

The overriding impression of the months at sea is peace – peace broken only by an occasional crisis, and by the disturbing habits of passengers. This I can well understand from my own observation. Arabs can sometimes be excitable, either individually or in crowds, but they have an enviable gift of living calmly together in little groups, taking life easily without getting on each other's nerves. (The man who lost his temper in the *Najeeb* was an Indian, not an Arab.) The secret of it is that, however tough they may be, they remain sincerely religious people, more aware than average Christians of the immediate presence of their God. There is not much time for enmity to grow or resentment to fester when everything stops five times a day for prayers, and everyone is enjoined at those times to put all worldly thoughts from his mind; and in a dhow at sea the prayers are observed as strictly as anywhere – more strictly than in the towns, where many people neglect them nowadays. Besides, to be at sea, especially under sail, has always given men, not only Moslems, a sense of their own smallness and the power and mercy of their God. The crew of a dhow, good men and bad, is united at times of prayer; it has the essence of a religious group. So united, the men work together with a minimum of orders, or none at all.

The second impression is informality. Most ships are run by rules, and strictly to time. But there are no rules in a dhow – or if there are, they are so well understood and accepted that no outsider is aware of them. Without an official clock, nobody cares what time it is, except to know when it is time for prayers, and that is determined by the sun, not by the clock. Nor do they know or care what day it is, except to know when the month of Ramadhan begins and ends. So there are no watches in the nautical sense. When there is

work to do, everyone does it, and when there is not they sleep, and Friday, the day of rest, is the same as any other. When the man at the wheel is tired there is always somebody else to take over. This way of doing things may be easier, of course, because everyone is there, present and visible on deck, whether he is asleep or not; nobody has to be called from below, because there is nowhere below that he could be. It is also easier because Arabs sleep soundly but lightly, and wake up instantly and apparently cheerfully whenever they are needed.

In this and in many other ways, life in a dhow resembles life in the desert – or so it seems to an outsider. The captain of a dhow is a sophisticated man; but the crew are the same kind of people as Bedouin, who also live for most of their lives in small communities. The captain has unquestioned authority, like any minor sheik of a nomad tribe. But neither a captain nor a sheik lives apart or is unapproachable; he rules by virtue of tradition and uses his authority within the bounds the

tradition sets for him. Besides ruling, the minor sheik is expected to find good pasture for his people's flocks, and the captain to find good chances of profit for his crew. Neither is expected to be infallible, but both are expected to be good at their job. If they are not, the sheik will find he has no following, and the captain will have no crew.

For all the peace and informality, life in a dhow is extremely hard – again like life in the desert. Not many people would be willing to live without any physical comfort, unless they had been brought up to it and knew of it from generations of ancestral memory. There is no comfort on a dhow except the warmth of the sun, and often too much of that. Not even eating is a comfort. The food is sufficient, but nothing more – tea, dates, unleavened bread, and rice with a flavouring of fish and ghee and peppers, and sometimes, mostly in harbour, a sheep or goat that is slaughtered on the foredeck. Meals are eaten as quickly as possible, in silence, as a necessity. Nor is there

any recreation, physical or mental, unless one counts the pleasure men get from contemplating the contents of their sea-chests, and telling each other stories, and hearing or reciting passages from the Koran, and lingering over hashish or tobacco. When a dhow puts to sea, it puts the world behind it.

There is always another side to peace, and that is monotony. Anyone with a restless mind might find a long dhow voyage unbearably boring – more boring than a voyage in a ship that was run by rules, where even the changing of a watch relieves monotony. I do not think a simple Arab knows what boredom is: it only starts if education or a city life has given him the doubtful blessing of a restless mind. By nature, he does not yearn for anything but sameness, and once in a while, as a rare event to remember or anticipate, a feast or perhaps a battle. He is content to live slowly, whether he is a nomad in the desert or on the sea. But the loss of this contentment may be part of the price the Arabs have to pay for the wealth of oil.

The Future

In these days, any outsider who tries to predict the future of anything in Arabia is likely to make a fool of himself. Forty years ago, people were saying the dhows were finished, and they are still going strong. It remains very hard to imagine an economic future for anything so archaic as a dhow; but the owners and captains of dhows have always shown an instinct for survival, and perhaps they will go on finding work that a dhow can do better than any more modern ship. I hope they will. It is useless to grieve for the end of a human craft, even if it has lasted 4500 years. But studying dhows and the people who build and sail them, one cannot help growing fond of them, and so one wishes them well.

But I will risk one suggestion: that this building and sailing of dhows may soon drift out of Arab hands and be left to their poorer neighbours. Everywhere in the rich Arab states, one can see this tendency already. In the boatyards, especially those at the southern end of the Gulf, the master-builders and foremen are still Arabs – though mostly growing old – but practically all the skilled manual workers are Indian or Pakistani. The big new boom *Najeeb* which we photographed under sail was built in India because it was cheaper: high wages, linked to a high cost of living, have pushed up the price of new dhows, like most other things in Arabia. Again, most of the big dhows in a place like Dubai are not Arab at all,

but Indian or Pakistani; and even in an Arab dhow with an Arab captain, half of the crew is likely to be foreign. The fact is that any Arab can make more money and live more at ease by staying ashore; it is natural if they are reluctant to go away on six-month voyages and miss the chances for well-paid jobs at home. As the Bahraini said to me, young Arabs now expect to set up their own businesses – and who is to blame them?

Yet seamanship and craftsmanship cannot survive without apprentices. So, although dhows may continue to trade for a long time yet, I foresee the end of Arab dhows, except the small ones that work around the shores. Big ones will be built and owned and manned by Pakistanis, Indians and Africans, and only perhaps by Arabs in the corners of Arabia that have not discovered oil.

That is in trade. There is another possibility. When I was in the boatyard at Ras al Khaimar I met an elegant young Arab who was inspecting the shu'ais and told me he was thinking of buying one. I asked him what he was going to do with it, because he was obviously not a fisherman, and he said he wanted to use it for picnics. Here perhaps is a chance for the dhow-builder's art. Arabs have a hot and dusty land, and a blue, enchanting sea: the rich young men in the coastal towns will surely take to yachting when things settle down a bit and they have more leisure at home. They may be tempted by the kind of fast fibre-glass motor yachts one sees in other rich parts of the world, but some may cherish the much more beautiful shapes of the old shu'ais and sambuks; and some of the dhow-builders' yards, like most of the yards of Britain, may be able to live by building pleasure-boats.

At any rate, if the dhows are doomed to disappear from the seas, the Arabs will not make the same mistake we made in the past, of letting our ships rot away and failing to preserve a few of each era – so that now we do not even know exactly what they were like. In the midst of the greatest convulsion of wealth that has ever hit any race, Arabs have begun to preserve what relics they can of their cultural history. They are building museums, and most of the coastal capitals have kept a few of the smaller dhows as exhibits.

It is no business of mine to tell the Arabs what they ought to do; they are pestered too much by advisers, good and bad. But if they decide to set up a huge museum of all the kinds of dhows, I can assure them it will interest their western visitors, not only their own grandchildren; for we shall be able to see in it the nearest things in the world to the ships we allowed to vanish, the medieval cogs, the galleons, the caravels and East Indiamen.